CELEBRATING
THE RITES OF ADULT
INITIATION
PASTORAL REFLECTIONS

Font and Table Series

The *Font and Table Series* offers pastoral perspectives on Christian baptism, confirmation and eucharist.

Other titles in the series are:

A Catechumenate Needs Everybody: Study Guides for Parish Ministers

At that Time: Cycles and Seasons in the Life of a Christian

Baptism Is a Beginning

The Church Speaks about Sacraments with Children:
Baptism, Confirmation, Eucharist, Penance

Confirmation: A Parish Celebration

Confirmed as Children, Affirmed as Teens

Finding and Forming Sponsors and Godparents

Guide for Sponsors

How Does a Person Become a Catholic?

How to Form a Catechumenate Team

Issues in the Christian Initiation of Children

Parish Catechumenate: Pastors, Presiders, Preachers

Welcoming the New Catholic

When Should We Confirm? The Order of Initiation

Related and available through Liturgy Training Publications:

The Rite of Christian Initiation of Adults (Ritual Edition)

The Rite of Christian Initiation of Adults (Study Edition)

Catechumenate: A Journal of Christian Initiation

CELEBRATING
THE RITES OF ADULT
INITIATION
PASTORAL REFLECTIONS

RITA FERRONE

EDWARD FOLEY

MARK R. FRANCIS

KATHLEEN HUGHES

MICHAEL JONCAS

CATHERINE MOWRY LACUGNA

MARGUERITE MAIN

JAMES MOUDRY

RONALD A. OAKHAM

EDITED BY

VICTORIA M. TUFANO

LITURGY TRAINING PUBLICATIONS

ACKNOWLEDGMENTS

All references to the *Rite of Christian Initiation of Adults*
(RCIA) are based on the text and the paragraph numbers of the 1988
edition: © 1985, International Commission on English in the Liturgy;
© 1988, United States Catholic Conference.

Liturgy Training Publications,
1800 North Hermitage Avenue, Chicago IL 60622-1101
Editorial: 312-486-8970
Orders: 1-800-933-1800

Editorial Assistance: David Philippart, Theresa Pincich, Lorraine Schmidt
Art: Linda Ekstrom
Design: Jill Smith
Typesetter: Mark Hollopeter

Printed in the United States of America

Library of Congress Cataloging-in-Publication Data

Celebrating the rites of adult initiation: pastoral reflections/edited by Victoria
   M. Tufano; authors, Rita Ferrone . . . [et al.].
     p.   cm. — (Font and table series)
   ISBN 0-929650-45-X : $7.95
   1. Catholic Church. *Ordo initianionis Christianae adultorum.*
   2. Catholic Church — Liturgy. 3. Initiation rites — Religious aspects —
Catholic Church.   I. Tufano, Victoria M., 1952 - . II. Ferrone,
Rita.   III. Series.
BX2045.I55C45 1992
268'.434 — dc20   91-40485
                                                CIP

CONTENTS

Introduction

As this book is being published, a little more than three years have passed since the revised *Rite of Christian Initiation of Adults* was mandated for use in the dioceses of the United States, a little more than 17 years since the provisional text became available in English, and 20 years since the Latin text was promulgated. In the lifecycle of Catholic rituals, the rites leading to the sacraments of initiation are still in their infancy. True, they have long existed in the archives of Christian history. But over the centuries, their rhythms and movements have been bred out of the bones of Christian worshipers, falling into disuse and all but forgotten.

Over the past two decades, we have begun to try out these ancient patterns and to add to them rhythms and movements more familiar to modern worshipers. The results sometimes have been awkward, sometimes graceful, and occasionally inspired. Almost always, however, they have afforded a glimpse of a mystery beyond themselves, of a reality inexpressible in words alone.

Eventually these rites will become familiar parts of our repertoire of worship. They will shape our understanding of who we are as baptized Christians, of what our mission in the world is, of what it means to accept the cross and the word, and what it means to share bread and wine. The experience of these rites already has begun to influence the way we prepare candidates for marriage, for confirmation and first communion, and even for profession of religious vows.

VICTORIA M.
TUFANO

Readers of this book, particularly those new to the ministry of initiation, are encouraged to have a copy of the

Rite of Christian Initiation of Adults nearby while reading. Each text has an order and integrity that is as much a part of it as the words and gestures. Like a musician who would improvise on a musical text, one who would adapt a ritual must first know and understand it as it is given in the text. Appropriate ritual adaptations are grounded in this understanding of the texts and in the understanding of the community that will celebrate the rites.

This book is arranged according to the order that these rites normally occur. Kathleen Hughes examines the meaning and shape of the rite of acceptance into the order of catechumens. Although it is not usually considered one of the rites of the initiation process, the liturgy of the word is the most important rite for catechumens. James Moudry offers his vision of a renewed liturgy of the word and its power to form catechumens and faithful alike. Edward Foley and Marguerite Main examine two of the rites of the period of the catechumenate that often seem, as Foley suggests, "restored more in theory than in practice": the minor exorcisms and the blessings of catechumens. Ronald A. Oakham shares his perspective on the rites of sending catechumens for election and of sending candidates to the bishop for recognition. Mark R. Francis, Michael Joncas and Rita Ferrone each offer a unique perspective on one of the three scrutinies, and Catherine Mowry Lacugna unfolds the riches of the presentations of the Creed and the Lord's Prayer. Kathleen Hughes brings the book to a close by exploring what it means to choose a baptismal name, one of the preparation rites that may be celebrated on Holy Saturday.

Most of these eleven reflections on the rites leading to the sacraments of initiation were published originally in *Catechumenate: A Journal of Christian Initiation*. The authors are scholars, teachers and pastoral leaders who have worked with these rites, listened to their rhythms and helped others move to them, enter into them and adapt them. These reflections provide historical and theological bases for understanding the rites as they are given. Working from this foundation, the authors offer guidance and suggestions for the adapting and enactment of these rites.

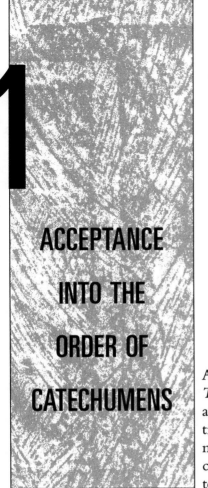

1

ACCEPTANCE INTO THE ORDER OF CATECHUMENS

Arnold Van Gennep, in his classic work *The Rites of Passage,* was the first to articulate what all of us know instinctively, namely, that significant moments of human transition or passage can be extremely difficult, sometimes terrifying and always unpredictable and unsettling. The passage moments that Van Gennep included are: experiences of territorial passage such as movement across thresholds or fixed boundaries; change of status associated, for example, with tribal puberty rites; the seasonal changes of agricultural patterns for cycles related to the phases of the moon; times of life crises such as birth, betrothal, acute illness and dying.

What Van Gennep discovered was that all these passage moments shared certain common features. He detected a classic ritual pattern that appeared to accompany every change of place, of state, of social position and of human maturation. Van Gennep named this pattern "rites of passage," and he postulated that all significant human passages have a sequence in common: a *separation* phase comprising symbolic behavior that expresses detachment from an earlier fixed point in the social structure; a *liminal* or marginal phase during which the experiences of persons undergoing the passage are

KATHLEEN
HUGHES

no longer what they were—but not yet what they will become; and a *reincorporation* phase in which the passage has been negotiated and the persons have attained a new place in the social structure.

Later theorists such as Victor Turner built on Van Gennep's insights, particularly by developing the critical, middle phase of passage, the experience of liminality. People who are undergoing significant passage experiences—whether, for example, becoming engaged, entering religious life, joining the marines, beginning a new profession or moving into a different culture—have several things in common. They all fall outside normal structural arrangements. They live "at the edges" or "in the cracks." They are—using a term to which Turner gives technical meaning—"betwixt and between," not yet part of a new social system, but having lost their moorings in the old. Their status is ambiguous; they experience dispossession; they are vulnerable; they feel stripped of all rank as they pass through a symbolic domain with few attributes of past or future.

The guidance of others and the celebration of ritual at key moments are crucial to a successful negotiation of the passage. In rites of initiation, for example, one learns a new way of life only with the help of sponsors and guides. One learns "the wisdom of the elders" less by what they say than by closely associating with those who have themselves already traversed the passage successfully. At the same time, ritual is uniquely able to mediate the same critical passage moments. Ritual helps individuals come to terms with what is happening in their lives by giving it a name and bringing it to symbolization. In a sense, a ritual acts like a fulcrum, first bringing what is already experienced to full public expression and at the same time negotiating the beginnings of a new passage and a deeper commitment to the process.

The Rite of Acceptance as a Rite of Separation

These anthropological insights are crucial for the understanding and celebration of the rite of acceptance into the order of catechumens. This rite would be classified by Van Gennep as a rite of separation, the first of a complex series of ritual moments in the Christian initiation of adults that will help the inquirer negotiate the passage from outsider to insider, from solitary individual to member of a community, from unbeliever to believer.

Acceptance into the order of catechumens stands at the juncture of "separation" and "liminality." After its celebration, an inquirer is no longer an inquirer, but not yet a Christian. The inquirer becomes a "catechumen"—one to be taught—and enters into the phase of liminality described earlier as living on the margins, dispossessed, betwixt and between. In the rite of acceptance, an inquirer makes his or her intentions public for the first time and crosses a threshold—quite literally—into uncharted territory, a passage experience as unsettling and ambiguous as any of the passages named previously. Not until the Easter Vigil with its "rites of reincorporation" will the inquirer complete the passage in the celebration of the initiatory sacraments and find a new "home" as a Christian believer.

During the interim, the liminal phase, the inquirer-become-catechumen will live as a nomad, betwixt and between. The catechumen's status will be ambiguous; the catechumen will feel vulnerable. However well educated or professionally competent, the catechumen will feel like a child needing to learn a new language and a new way of life, ignorant of the basics but sometimes not even knowing the right questions to ask. Chasms will open between the catechumen, the family and the friends, yet new relationships will only gradually be formed. He or she will negotiate the passage from inquirer to believer with the help of sponsors and guides whose role, in light of the vulnerable state of the catechumen, cannot be underestimated. Sponsors gradually communicate "the wisdom of the elders," patiently invite the catechumen to a gospel way of life in the midst of others and, in some measure, serve as a mooring for the catechumen's fragile barque.

The foregoing suggests the importance of the rite of acceptance at this critical juncture in the life of an inquirer. It raises important questions at the same time: When and how should this rite be celebrated to achieve its full ritual potential?

When the Time Is Right

There is an intriguing statement in the *Rite of Christian Initiation of Adults* (RCIA) specifying the appropriate time for the celebration of this welcoming ritual: "The rite of acceptance into the order of catechumens is to take place when the time is right" (28). The reader then is referred to a previous section where it is stated that the candidate must have had "sufficient time to conceive an initial faith and to show the first signs of conversion" (18). This seems to suggest that "the time is right" for celebration when there is something to celebrate, namely, initial faith and the beginnings of conversion. Little more is said.

But what if we didn't have any commentary at all? What if all that the *Rite of Christian Initiation of Adults* contained were a series of rites without pastoral notes? The rite itself is the richest source of "commentary" on the human religious experience of the inquirer. The rite suggests the content of the discernment of readiness. Whether "the time is right" for celebration may be discovered by examining the rite and posing certain questions: What are we celebrating? What does the rite presume has already happened in the life of the inquirer? What experience does it ritualize? Once an inquirer becomes a catechumen, what is he or she prepared to do? What hopes does the rite express? What pledges does it make? What demands does it place on various ministers, and what role does it assign to the community as a whole?

If it is true that ritual helps an individual negotiate difficult moments of transition, the full meaning of the passage must be ritually expressed. The rite of acceptance tells us that the right time for celebration is that graced moment when an inquirer is ready to stand at the door of the church and knock. An inquirer, according to the rite, is ready to make private intentions public, to begin a journey of conversion, to associate with a community of believers, to open oneself to the crucified Christ, to become a disciple with all that demands, to respond daily more generously to the invitation of the Spirit and to embrace a way of life. This much can be ascertained from the ritual activity of inquirer and community.

The language of the rite further suggests that the religious experience that brings an inquirer to the point of readiness will be unique to each one, as will be the way that he or she responds to the initiative of God. This is demonstrated clearly in the variety of prayers provided to elicit a candidate's "first acceptance of the gospel," a moment when the candidate says clearly and publicly that he or she desires to embrace a gospel way of life, the demands of which also are spelled out.

In one prayer (52 A), all of creation is revelatory of God. What has brought the inquirer this far is named "following God's light." The metaphor for the catechumenate is that of a journey made under the guidance of Christ—the way of faith daily deepened as one comes to believe in Christ with all one's heart, learning to trust in his wisdom.

A second prayer (52 B), though addressed to God our Creator, is more focused on Christ as God's faithful witness, Christ whom we are able to recognize because we are enlightened by God's grace. This prayer names the experience of first faith as recognition that Christ has come; the catechumenate will be devoted to hearing his word "in our company." In this prayer, the inquirer's acceptance of the gospel is acceptance of a way of life in the midst of others.

The third optional text is a prayer that is less evocative and more explicitly demanding than the others. Weaving scriptural phrases together, it states the basic kerygma that must be accepted by any inquirer at this juncture: knowledge of God and of the Son who is dead, risen and exalted Lord of life. This third formula (52C) suggests that the impulse that brings a candidate to this ritual moment is the desire to become a disciple. Then, in strong "must" language, it states what the work of the catechumen is: to be guided to the fullness of truth, to put on the mind of Christ and to pattern one's life on the teachings of the gospel.

Other optional texts could be written, of course, suggesting other metaphors for the journey, other ways of conceiving the relationship with the Hound of Heaven, other ways of naming the covenant that here is being forged. Suffice it to say that the verbal language of the rite is porous, often introduced by the phrase "in these or similar words." The verbal language attempts to name the reality of this ritual moment: A unique individual is responding to an invitation from One who is wholly other. The mystery of God's grace escapes all of our fragile attempts to conceptualize it. The rite of acceptance tempts us to multiply words in our desire to find those expressions best able to capture the uniqueness of an inquirer's experience of this passage. Yet liturgical language strains and cracks under such pressure. Only the symbolic language of movement and gesture will suffice to gather up and express to the full this moment of passage. Thank God for the nonverbal language of the rites.

The Shape of the Rite

Though the *Rite of Christian Initiation of Adults* contains a fairly elaborate outline for the rite of acceptance, I would like to propose a simpler structure to highlight the ritual action:

Assembling

Covenanting

Signing

Processing

Listening

Praying

Sending

We will look at these in turn.

Assembling (RCIA, 48–49)   The gathering of the community and the inquirers preferably takes place outside the church. While space, inclement weather, disability or some other circumstance might dictate otherwise, the act of crossing the threshold is a crucial ritual statement. These candidates are seeking entrance into the church; here they act out that desire. They "stand at the door and knock." As inquirers, they do not simply experience first faith or conversion in solitude but come to recognize that they are being invited to ecclesial faith and to participation in a body of believers, all of whom are on a journey of conversion.

Crossing the threshold has been named by many participants, after the fact, as one of the two most significant moments in this rite.

The community in the person of its ministers "goes to meet the candidates" (48), a highly symbolic action suggesting that the church goes out to meet these men and women, almost as did the prodigal father, welcoming them in the midst of their journey "home." It is the role of the presider to express the joy of the community in the decision of the inquirers and, in his greeting of the candidates, to allude to the particular circumstances of the candidates' journeys that have brought them to this threshold moment (49). The presumption is that the presider of this rite knows the candidates individually, has listened to their stories, values their individual responses to God's initiative in their lives and is able to speak a word from the heart as he invites them to come forward.

Covenanting (RCIA, 50–53)   Once assembled, the inquirers and the community speak to each other of their hopes and promises.

The inquirers begin. The rite makes optional whether the candidates are called by name or are asked to give their names to the community (50). One might ask if it really matters which option is selected. Yet it would seem preferable for inquirers to speak their own names and, in so doing, to entrust themselves to the community. At the threshold, candidates are requesting admission. While "What is your name?" may sound a bit foolish, "Would you give your name to the community?" may seem more inviting but still places the initiative on the candidates. Furthermore, names will be called out at the time of election, which will take place a year later (130). At that point, individuals are able to be "called by name" because they are known by those who have been on the journey with them. In the rite of acceptance, the same "knowledge"—as the Hebrew *knowledge of a name* implies a personal bond—cannot yet be assumed.

After the naming, the opening dialogue continues (50). As with the greeting, the dialogue demands that the presider be able to draw out from the candidates, each in his or her own words, what has brought them to this threshold and that he base his follow-up questions on the actual responses he receives. The dialogue in the rite is simply a model of the exchange that takes place here. Some candidates may be reticent before the assembly; preparation for this moment is crucial lest canned answers prevent a personal expression of intention.

The candidates' first acceptance of the gospel (52), treated earlier, follows. Simplicity and brevity are in order.

The sponsors respond. The sponsors' role now is simply defined: They act as the candidates' *witnesses to the community* by presenting the candidates to the community, and they will act as *witnesses for the community* and all it holds dear by helping the candidates find and follow Christ. The rite provides a model formula to elicit the sponsors' acceptance of this ministry and their affirmation of the candidates' readiness. It may be adapted as appropriate so that the same warmth of approach to the candidates is mirrored again here. In the adaptation, allusion to the role of the community in the initiatory process is appropriate.

A prayer follows the sponsors' declaration of readiness to assume their role. The language is sufficiently ambiguous: "These are your servants" could refer to the sponsors or to the candidates. In the context of "affirmation by sponsors and assembly," the prayer might be interpreted as a prayer of praise and thanksgiving for those willing to assume the ministry of sponsor. The content of the prayer is thanksgiving and praise that God's initiative has been met by faithful response on the part of God's servants. The provisional text of the rite more clearly indicated that this prayer actually refers to the candidates. It is an odd prayer, in an odd location in the rite. By gesture, perhaps even by a word of transition and introduction, the prayer would find a more congenial home. For example, after the sponsors and the community have promised to "help these candidates find and follow Christ," the presider might say: "Join me, then, in giving thanks for God's action in the lives of these men and women."

Signing (RCIA, 54–57)   The signing of the senses with the cross of Christ is a high point of this rite. Inquirers have stated their intention to begin a journey, to hear the word in the midst of the community, to become disciples. Now their whole being is marked by the cross, for strength, as a sign of love, as a challenge to deeper knowledge and discipleship. The signing of all of the senses (56), instead of the option of signing only the forehead, suggests that the time of the catechumenate is not simply about acquiring sufficient knowledge but rather about engaging in a process of listening and hearing, of seeing and speaking, of experiencing Christ's presence and of bearing Christ's yoke, of making all activities a living worship, of making all journeys and resting places the place of Christ's manifestation.

The concluding prayer further elaborates this moment. There are two texts from which to choose. The first (57 A) underscores the power of the cross to seal the grace that has begun in these candidates and to hold out the hope of glory and rebirth in the Easter waters. The second (57 B) names the cross the sign of life and petitions God to transform these candidates into witnesses of God's saving power as they persevere in following Christ.

Processing (RCIA, 60)   It seems fitting, after a rite of such power, that the cross head the procession into the church. It is the cross of Christ that is named our life and our hope. The way of Christ crucified is what catechumens follow. At this moment, when they are beginning to walk in the way of Christ, that cross that was traced on their bodies now stands at the beginning of their journey and opens up the path they follow.

The presider invites the catechumens into the church. The model invitation is simple and to the point: "Come into the church to share with us at the table of God's word." These or other words may be employed along with some gesture of invitation. Bearing in mind that this is a critical juncture for the catechumens, a very deliberate and perhaps slightly more elaborate invitation may be appropriate for this "threshold moment." The focus of the invitation is twofold: Enter the church; hear the word. Both deserve attention. The ritual procession is marked by solemnity and formality as catechumens enter the church and join themselves to the household of the faith in whose midst, step by step, they will complete their journey.

Listening (RCIA, 61–63)   An odd rubric follows. The celebrant is told to speak to the candidates about the dignity of God's word (61). One would hope that the words, "dignity of God's word," are tautological. "The dignity of God's word" will be reflected in the care for the lectionary and the book of the gospels, the preparation to assure excellent proclamation, the marks of reverence (candles, incense) surrounding the gospel procession and proclamation—and, it needs to be added, the care with which the homilist prepares a homily that will assist in the unfolding of the scriptures, "that necessary source of nourishment of the Christian life" for believers and catechumens alike *(General Instruction of the Roman Missal, 41).*

In other words, the catechumens need less to be "instructed" about the dignity of God's word than to feel it in their bones because of the way others act out that dignity. Rather than "instruction," a presider needs to recall how priceless is this moment when, for the first time, the community opens up its treasure, the word of God, in the presence of the catechumens, and how their ears have just been signed that "they may hear the voice of the Lord."

While one set of texts is proposed (RCIA, 62), a community is free to select any lectionary texts. In the set of proposed texts, only a first reading, response, verse before the gospel and gospel text are included. The presumption here appears to be that the rite of acceptance will take place on a weekday, but that, too, needs to be considered.

What we are ritualizing is that these inquirers now are making a first public declaration of their intent to become members of the church. At the same time, the church receives them and accepts and blesses their intention. This mutual "covenanting" will be the richer as more members of the community are present to receive this declaration and to welcome inquirers to sit at the table of God's word with them. That seems to suggest that a Sunday celebration is most apt for the rite, in which case the Sunday readings are chosen.

Praying (RCIA, 65)   The word of God stirs the hearts of all present and draws out the community's longings for the world, the church, the dispossessed and the catechumens in its assembly. The optional set of intercessions included in the rite highlights the journey these men and women have begun under the gentle guidance of God, a journey into ever-deeper knowledge of Christ until that great Easter day of new birth and renewal in the Spirit. The community asks generosity for the catechumens, and for itself it asks the gifts of unfailing support, faithful witness and responsiveness to the needs of others. These intercessions serve simply as a model for thoughtful adaptation to the circumstances and needs of particular assemblies.

Sending (RCIA, 66–67)   The intercessory prayer is sealed with a prayer over the catechumens (66) that anticipates their need for God's continued gentle presence on their journey as they are gradually transformed into the likeness of Christ. Then they are dismissed. The same reverence and hospitality that marked the assembling of the community will mark its dismissal of these newest members of the household of the faith.

Conclusion

T. S. Eliot wrote in his poem *The Dry Salvages:* "We had the experience but missed the meaning." It is a line worth reflecting on as we conclude this commentary on the rite of acceptance.

There are at least three instances when we might "miss the meaning" of a rite. The first is to celebrate a ritual, this one or any other, prematurely. The power of the ritual is in bringing to expression what is already going on in the lives of those celebrating it. While rites can deepen experience, they cannot create it. In the case of the rite of acceptance, the ritual would be premature until an inquirer is ready to make a public declaration that he or she desires to embrace a gospel way of life. In many cases, the full meaning of that declaration will not be apparent to the inquirer who still is looking for a language and searching for words to name the whispers of God's grace and understand the stirrings of his or her own heart. Indeed, the full meaning of that declaration will unfold only over a lifetime.

Nevertheless, readiness for public declaration, however halting, is important, as is the willingness, in this rite of separation, to leave the past behind. Candidates may name their desire "conversion" or "disciple-ship" or "longing to know Christ." Candidates may have no words yet for their experience. But they must exhibit a willingness to be signed by the cross of Christ and to open their hearts to the words of the gospel— or else the rite is premature.

We also might "miss the meaning" if we become enamored of the multiplication of words. The rite of acceptance often invites a presider to adapt or compose a text. It is a great temptation, always to be resisted, to increase the verbal language of a rite. It tends to drown the primary symbols. At a time of such importance, words can sound so pedantic. An example is found in one of the introductions to the signing of the cross (55 B). Referring to the candidates' statement of intention, the presider says: "Dear candidates, your answers mean that you wish to share our life and hope in Christ." The candidates' answers must stand on their own. They *mean* so much more than we can capture in words. In the composition of texts and in the ritual dialogue that takes place more spontaneously, simplicity and brevity may be excellent rules of thumb to let the primary symbols and ritual actions, unencumbered by useless explanations, speak their particular richness.

Finally, we might "miss the meaning" in our very attempts to invest symbols with more meaning. I refer to the optional rites of giving candidates a cross after the signing with the cross of Christ (59) and a book of the scriptures after the hearing of the word of God (64). In this instance, a multiplication of symbols could trivialize the two most powerful symbols of the rite of acceptance. Is it possible that we domesticate the power of the cross by hanging it around our necks as a piece of jewelry, that we make it *our* cross—even talisman—rather than that of the crucified Christ? Similarly, does it make sense to give out Bibles and thereby possibly imply that the word of God is captured between the covers of a book? Again, do we dilute the word; do we blunt the power of the two-edged sword?

Too soon, too many words, too many symbols—it is so easy to have an experience "but miss the meaning." We cannot let it happen— not in this rite of separation so critical at the beginning of a long and rich passage. But a rite of acceptance, carefully executed, fulfills a profound ritual need for candidate and community alike. Eliot knew it well:

> We had the experience but missed the meaning,
> And approach to the meaning restores the experience
> In a different form, beyond any meaning
> We can assign to happiness.

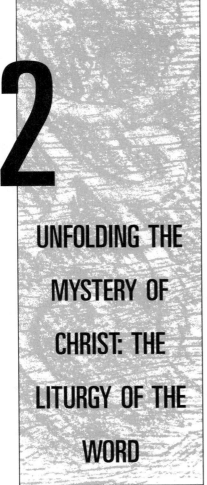

2

UNFOLDING THE MYSTERY OF CHRIST: THE LITURGY OF THE WORD

When one lists the real accomplishments of the liturgical reform initiated by Vatican II and the *Constitution on the Sacred Liturgy,* the reform of the lectionary certainly will rank close to the top. Its shortcomings notwithstanding, the revised lectionary offers the church a richness that it had not known before. The lectionary is a tangible sign of the Catholic Church's renewed commitment to the primacy of the word of God in the life of its members.

We have learned, however, that a reformed book does not a renewed liturgy make. The lectionary may be brilliantly conceived, but of itself it cannot release the word of God into our midst. A liturgy of the word can do that. But celebrating the liturgy of the word so that the power of the word is released among the worshipers is not an obvious or easy action. It is my intent in this chapter to reflect on the celebration of the liturgy of the word in the Sunday eucharistic assembly. I do this with the hope that pausing to look again at what we are doing or not doing may reward us with better insights into the liturgy of the word and motivate us to effect better celebrations. The reason for taking a look at the liturgy of the word in this book is the vital role the word of God plays

JAMES
MOUDRY

in the conversion of those journeying to the initiation sacraments and beyond.

Christian Initiation and Celebrations of the Word

The initiation of catechumens takes place within the community of the faithful, who provide example and help for the catechumens by joining them in reflection on the paschal mystery and by renewing their own conversion (RCIA, 4). The most public expression of this common reflection on the paschal mystery occurs in the assembly's celebration of the Sunday eucharist. Catechumens are invited to be a part of the liturgy of the word. After the homily, they are dismissed for catechetical reflection on those proclaimed scriptures, while the rest of the community goes on to the liturgy of the table, which renders manifest the paschal Christ among us.

The liturgy of the word is the preeminent celebration of the word, but it is not the only such celebration. Recalling what the *Rite of Christian Initiation of Adults* says about celebrations of the word will help us to understand what is distinctive about the liturgy of the word at Sunday eucharist and the weight that it is asked to bear in the formation of the catechumens.

Not all celebrations of the word are the liturgy of the word. The RCIA distinguishes between celebrations of the word that support the catechesis leading "to an appropriate acquaintance with dogmas and precepts" and "to a profound sense of the mystery of salvation" (75.1), and celebrations of the word that are a part of the liturgical rites belonging to the catechumenal journey (75.3). Among the latter are the celebrations of the liturgy of the word with the faithful at Sunday Mass, celebrations that prepare them "for their eventual participation in the liturgy of the eucharist" (75.3).

This distinction is made more clear in the description of celebrations of the word of God during the period of the catechumenate (81–89). The rite speaks of celebrating word services on Sunday as a way to teach the catechumens how to keep holy the Lord's Day. Then it adds, "Gradually the catechumens should be admitted to the first part of the celebration of the Sunday Mass," namely, the liturgy of the word (83).

The significance of these distinctions is twofold. First, they make clear that there is a difference between celebrations of the word and the liturgy of the word. The latter refers to what we do in the eucharistic assembly, particularly on Sunday. Second, they emphasize that among the celebrations of the word, the liturgy of the word at eucharist holds a unique place both for the formation of the catechumens and the ongoing conversion of the faithful. The uniqueness in question has to do with the nature of the eucharistic celebration. The word that is proclaimed in the eucharistic assembly interacts with the meal ritual in a distinct and preeminent fashion. It is not just another "celebration of the word" in support of catechesis.[1]

Liturgy of the Word and the Table

The goal of the initiation journey is not merely to bring the catechumens to the baptismal font; the goal is to bring them to the eucharistic table. It is participation at the table each Sunday that is the distinctive characteristic of membership in the Catholic Christian community. It is from the table that the faithful are sent forth to do Christ's work of bringing the reign of God into the world. For a full member to join the Sunday assembly and not partake in the eucharistic meal is to abort the transformative process. That awareness is what makes participation in the Sunday eucharist so painful for those who, for whatever reason, do not or cannot come to the table.

Some of the same sense of incompleteness will overtake the catechumens who are dismissed from the assembly following the liturgy of the word. Why? Because the liturgy of the word is linked to the liturgy of the table. In the words of the *Introduction to the Lectionary:*

> It can never be forgotten . . . that the divine word read and proclaimed by the church in the liturgy has as its one goal the sacrifice of the New Covenant and the banquet of grace, that is,

the eucharist. The celebration of Mass in which the word is heard and the eucharist is offered and received forms but one single act of divine worship. (10)

There is an inseparable union between the proclamation of the death of the Lord, the response of the people listening, and the offering through which Christ has confirmed the New Covenant in this blood. (44)

Studies of ritual have demonstrated the same connection. Story and festivity or ritual go together. Neither is complete without the other. Story names the group's significant life experience; ritual frames it and lifts it out for people to engage in symbolically. Contrary to current popular cultural perceptions, ritual is necessary for sustaining healthy group living.

Catechumens and the Liturgy of the Word

The rite of acceptance into the order of catechumens dramatically signs catechumens with the cross of Christ and invites them to come into the church "to share with us at the table of God's word" (60). The presider is directed to help them understand the dignity of God's word proclaimed and heard in the church (61), for this is the way the church nourishes and sustains them (47). As the catechumens are dismissed, the presider urges them to live according to the word of God they have just heard (67). If the gathering of the assembly and the liturgy of the word are done in the way the reformed liturgy intends, they should awaken in the catechumens a hunger for the eucharist with all the consequences noted earlier. That is why the manner of celebrating the liturgy of the word at the Sunday eucharist becomes so important for the formation of new members, and important, too, for the renewal of the whole worshiping community. All of this places tremendous pressure on the quality of our celebrations of the liturgy of the word. How well are we doing?

The Liturgy of the Word as Liturgy

The shortcomings of the celebration of the liturgy of the word are familiar and have been well chronicled.[2] The deficiencies are not, first of all, in the structure of the liturgy of the word but in our failure to understand and to implement pastorally what is being called for. Some of that failure is traceable to the difficulty we have in getting hold of the nature of the liturgy itself and, in particular, the nature of the liturgy of the word.

We need to recover the understanding and implications of two fundamental principles of the liturgical reform: the presence of Christ in the word proclaimed and his presence in the assembly itself (*Constitution on the Sacred Liturgy*, 7). Our experience of liturgy prior to Vatican II did not help us to claim these beliefs. That liturgy reinforced our belief in the presence of Christ in the Blessed Sacrament and in the person of the ordained priest. The liturgy generally was experienced as something done *for us* by the priest and from which we benefited. There was not much to suggest that the liturgy was being done *by us*. Similarly, the liturgy of the word was not included in the catechism description of the "principal parts of the Mass": the offertory, consecration and communion. The scripture readings were a kind of prelude to "the Mass," a less important "Mass of the Catechumens."

It is with difficulty that we understand the liturgy of the word as liturgy. Too often we think of it as a didactic prelude.[3] Evidence of that mind-set is the preoccupation of liturgy planners to uncover from the assigned biblical readings a theme that can be announced at the beginning of the Mass as the message that should be taken home from this liturgy and then played out in the musical selections, homily and general intercessions. That mind-set regards the liturgy of the word as a teaching-learning experience. This attitude is reinforced by an interpretation of "full, conscious and active" participation that says that the liturgy must be clear and simple so that the people will get the message—a posture that explains the curious anti-ritual bias of much contemporary parish worship. "Ritual" suggests to some a conceptual murkiness unfriendly to "instruction."

Although the liturgy of the word is liturgy and not instruction, it does form the attitudes of the worshipers. Why and how does this happen? Because the function of the liturgy of the word is to celebrate the mystery of Christ's presence among us. To make this point clear, the *Introduction to the Lectionary, 3*, recalls the gospel story of Jesus reading from the scriptures and then announcing, "Today this scripture passage is fulfilled in your hearing" (Luke 4:16–21). "The biblical text read by Jesus calls the hearers to ponder, not some event in past time, but One present in their midst."[4] The text and the preacher together reveal what God is doing here and now in this assembly of hearers. Proclamation serves not so much to inform as to reveal how the lives of the hearers are being interpreted because God is present and acting in this proclaimed word.

Celebrating the liturgy of the word as the mystery of Christ's presence among us requires our awareness and conviction that Christ is present in the assembly itself. Sacramental initiation configures believers to the person of Christ. From the moment the people assemble, they make manifest the Christ. Prior to doing anything ritually, they are, by assembling, the manifestation of the body of Christ.

Rigid adherence to the present structure of the introductory rite of the Mass can obscure this basic truth. Sometimes this rite is carried out in a way that exalts the person of the ordained presider over the presence of Christ in the assembly. Also, the rite often gives more attention to an introspective penitential moment than to the Lord of mercy who dwells with the assembly. A procession of special ministers into the assembly, complete with a "welcoming hymn" (a misnomer), can detract from the people's awareness that they are the Christ. Perhaps a more satisfying arrangement would be to begin with a call to worship with the ministers already in place, followed by a strong gathering song during which the book of the word is solemnly carried into the assembly and enthroned. The message of such a ritual is clear: It is God who gathers us and establishes us as members of Christ's body. This prepares the assembly to recognize what they are about in the proclamation of the word that follows.

Celebrating God's Presence

Because the liturgy is the act of Christ carried out in his body, the church, the assembly is both the hearer and the proclaimer of the word. As the assembled body of Christ, we tell the story of our identity in Christ. The biblical proclamation is not telling us *about* God speaking to us, it *is* God speaking to us. We are not seeking to be informed about a message God has for us but to be brought into communion with the God whose message is proclaimed. To celebrate the liturgy of the word is to celebrate God's presence in the proclaiming of the word. That should engender in us a sense of wonder and awe. What is going on is cause for rejoicing: We acclaim the presence of this holy God who speaks and tells us about ourselves by telling us about the divine presence in human history.

Understanding proclamation in the way just described yields insight into how to celebrate it. The context of proclamation must be public prayer and praise. A comparison with the liturgy of the eucharist can help. Frequently, people experience the liturgy of the eucharist — the praying of the eucharistic prayer and the communion rite — without being conscious of the specific meanings of what they hear or do. What they are conscious of is that they are involved in something holy, a sacred ritual that makes present the holy God. We need to work toward a similar awareness in the liturgy of the word. As important as the words of the story being proclaimed are, more important still is the consciousness among the worshipers that they are engaged in something holy, a sacred ritual in which they meet a God who speaks to them. The liturgy of the word needs full ritualization to evoke that sense of the sacred and to change the impression that what is happening is didactic communication.

Ritual Ingredients

The ritual ingredients of the liturgy of the word are ritual proclamation, musical acclamations, gesture and movement, silence, and ministers of proclamation and preaching who have an awareness of what ought to be happening. A word about ministries. The ministry of reader is a serious ministry, requiring spiritual development of the person as well as technical training in voice production and movement. Good intentions are not enough. The ability to read is not the same as the liturgical ministry of proclamation. Committing resources to the continuing development of readers ought to be a high priority in every parish. After all these years, the need appears as great as ever.

My second comment about these ministers has to do with who they are. For the most part, they are laypeople, women and men from the assembly acting out their baptismal empowerment as priests for holy worship. It is striking to note that except for the homily, the liturgical reform casts the ordained presider in the same role as the rest of the assembly during the liturgy of the word; he has no special tasks. Laypeople minister in the liturgy of the word regardless of the number of ordained priests who might be present. As representatives of the laity, the lay ministers affirm the entire assembly as co-celebrators of the liturgy, not spectators or responders to what others do for them.

The First and Second Readings

When the assembly sits after the opening prayer, a moment of silence follows before the reader approaches the lectern or place of the proclamation of the word. This place deserves to be suitably adorned in a way that matches the attention paid to the altar and its environs. The reader reads from a beautifully bound lectionary, not a missalette. We not only dishonor the word of God when we proclaim it from throwaway leaflets, but we dishonor the hearers. When we have a beautiful book for the presider's use (the sacramentary) but not for the ministry of reader, we are signaling to both reader and hearers that they are not important, and certainly not the very manifestation of Christ's presence. Nor are we supporting the truth that they are co-celebrators of the liturgy.

The reader holds the lectionary in his or her arms for the proclamation. This is holy storytelling, which needs to engage the hearers; it is not instruction from a book resting on a reading desk. The announcement that ends the reading, "This is the word of the Lord," refers to what has been proclaimed, not to the book. Hence the reader ought not raise the book aloft during those words. It confuses the lectionary with the proclamation of the word. The reader remains at the lectern for a few moments as the silence begins, and then leaves. The silence must be long enough for people to take seriously the invitation to ponder what they have heard proclaimed, a minimum of 30 seconds. The same procedure is followed for the second reading.

Responsorial Psalm

The responsorial psalm that follows the first reading has the potential to be one of the richest moments in the liturgy of the word. Potential, I say, because the idea of "response" in the liturgy is problematic. In recent liturgical history, making responses was synonymous with active participation and took the shape of the "dialogue Mass." Making responses meant reciting them because music was not an integral part of the dialogue-Mass experience.

All of this is problematic because the model of "making responses" assumes that the liturgy is something the priest carries out and to which the people give their assent by making responses. But Vatican II defines the liturgy as the action of the whole church, clergy and laity. Active participation is more than simply responding; it means engaging fully in an action that is not done for the people but by them. Thus, when the reformed liturgy of the word uses the language of "responses"—responsorial psalm, "Thanks be to God," and the gospel acclamations—we must consciously set aside the former connotations and move to an understanding that corresponds to the truth of active participation. The responses are ways in which the assembly assumes its celebrating role and acclaims the God who is present for these worshipers in the proclaimed word. Acclamation is more than assent; it means taking responsibility for what is happening.[5]

All of this is the backdrop for ritualizing the responsorial psalm. First of all, the responsorial psalm is a biblical reading, the proclamation of which belongs primarily to the assembly. Next, it is a psalm, and psalms are sung poetry. While the word "responsorial" does connote the idea of response to the reading just heard, it refers primarily to the manner in which the psalm is rendered, namely, in a back-and-forth fashion between cantor or choir and assembly. The psalm and its antiphon have been described, ingeniously in my judgment, as "an envelope or aura of prayer within which the reading occurs."[6] Its choice relates to the Hebrew Scripture that precedes it and to the text of the gospel that follows.

The singing of the antiphon and psalm is one way the people take hold of the word and make it their own. In a particular way, the antiphon sets the tone for the entire liturgy of the word. In light of that fact, a question: Might it be helpful to use the sung antiphon to introduce the first reading? Doing so could enhance the ritual character of the proclamation and at the same time serve as a hermeneutic (an interpretive context) for the readings that follow. We have learned that sung settings of the eucharistic prayer enhance its ritualization and draw the assembly into their most important prayer. There are parallel needs in the liturgy of the word.

The Gospel

After the second reading (again preceded and followed by significant periods of silence), the gospel follows. In Catholic tradition, the proclamation of the gospel in the liturgy of the word corresponds to the eucharistic prayer in the liturgy of the eucharist. It is a climactic moment recognizing Christ present and speaking with us.

Marks of honor suitable to that belief are in order. The gospel acclamation ends the silence and announces the beginning of the gospel procession. The gospel book is taken from the altar by the minister of the gospel (the deacon or, in his absence, the presider) and carried to the lectern with candles and incense. The gospel acclamation accompanies this action and should be synchronized so that when it is completed, the gospel minister is ready to greet the people and begin the gospel. If there is no gospel book, the reader of the second reading may bring the lectionary to the presider seated at the chair. He holds the book upright on his lap during the silence. When the acclamation begins, he stands and carries the book in procession to the lectern as previously described.

At the conclusion of the gospel proclamation, the acclamation may be repeated as a response to the words "This is the gospel of the Lord." Or it may be desirable to defer the singing of the acclamation until the completion of the homily and the silence that follows. This creates the sense that the homily is part of the proclamation and has the same purpose as it does, namely, to celebrate the divine presence in our midst in the proclaimed word. (It also may serve to challenge the homilist to rise to that purpose.) During the acclamation following the homily, the lectionary (or gospel book) may be carried to a place of honor and reverenced with incense.

The Homily

It is frequently said that there are three contexts for homily making: the exegetical, the contemporary and the liturgical. A word about the last in connection with our topic: The liturgical context refers first to the ritualization of the homily itself as part of a ritualized liturgy of the word. We already have noted the value of silence after the homily as well as the possible use of the gospel acclamation following the homily and during the enthronement of the book. In addition, preaching from the lectionary (or gospel book) open on the lectern or carried by the preacher, if he moves about while speaking, reinforces that the homily flows from the word of God proclaimed.

The second aspect of the liturgical context for homily making has to do with content. We noted earlier the intimate connection between the liturgy of the word and the table. Each Sunday homily ought to have some mystagogy in it, that is, a connecting of the assembly's ritual activity with the proclaimed word of the day. If true to what goes on in this liturgical assembly, the spoken and sung texts and the ritual actions will echo and enflesh the proclaimed word. It is important for the assembly to sense this connection so that they are encouraged to surrender their hearts and minds to the presence of Christ acting in this liturgy. The God of mystery is not accessed through logical discourse but through symbolic activity. A homily that awakens the hearers to the power of the symbols they are experiencing awakens them to the mystery of God hidden there.

The Formation of Catechumens

When catechumens are dismissed following the liturgy of the word, they are enjoined to live according to the word of God that they have just heard and to remain together to share their joy and spiritual experiences (RCIA, 67). What they have experienced is supposed to whet their appetite for the eucharist. The community of the faithful must ask itself, What have they heard? What have they experienced in our celebration of the word? Has it been an encounter with the God who speaks? Do they leave with a sense of wonder and awe, their hearts filled with joy? Do they know in their hearts that they have been with a community that delights in the presence of the holy God who tells them the story of their own lives by telling the story of how this God is present in human history? "By joining the catechumens in reflecting on the value of the paschal mystery and by renewing their own conversion, the faithful provide an example that will help the catechumens to obey the Holy Spirit more generously" (RCIA, 4).

We have two good reasons for enhancing the celebration of the liturgy of the word: the conversion of catechumens and our own conversion. The stakes are high. We can be certain that formation is occurring in each celebration of the word. The question is, is it good formation or bad, and are we willing to make it better?

The Christian community does a bold, indeed risky, thing when it introduces its particular story of the Christ into a human being's search for and experience of the Holy. If the church is to escape being presumptuous, it must do everything in its power to present that story in a way that symbolizes the possibility of an encounter with the divine. To settle for anything less than its best effort is to flirt with blasphemy.

Notes

[1] I am grateful to Carole Kastigar of the School of Divinity of the University of St. Thomas in St. Paul, Minnesota, for underlining the importance of this distinction from her work with proclamation of the word.

[2] Especially perceptive are the reflections of Ralph Keifer in his commentary in the form of essays on the lectionary for Mass, *To Hear and Proclaim* (Washington DC; NPM, 1983).

[3] *Ibid.,* 66 ff. For what follows I am indebted to Keifer's insights.

[4] *Ibid.,* 70.

[5] *Ibid.,* 82.

[6] R. Keifer, *To Give Thanks and Praise* (Washington DC: NPM, 1980), 123.

3

MINOR EXORCISMS

One of the happy faults of the *Rite of Christian Initiation of Adults* is the ritual overabundance of the period of enlightenment. Recall the enrollment of names, the scrutinies wed to the Year A readings of Lent, the *traditio symbolorum* and finally the rites of initiation embraced by the Easter Vigil. These are stirring, evocative moments that capture the imagination of catechumens and faithful alike.

In contrast to this intense period of election is the more amorphous period of the catechumenate. While the former, for example, presumes a particular time frame, the latter encompasses an indeterminate number of months or years, depending on the needs of the catechumens. The period of election has well-defined and well-articulated rites that are difficult to consider optional. The catechumenal period, in contrast, has simple, almost underdeveloped rites,[1] many of which are considered optional.[2]

Christian initiation is not a program of achievement culminating in graduation at the font but a process of conversion symbolized and motivated by a series of rites. Though these rites intensify during the period of enlightenment, they mark and mediate the whole of the catechumenal journey. For this to

EDWARD FOLEY

happen, we must respect and develop the ritual repertory for the entire catechumenate. One of the rites that requires such attention is that of the minor exorcisms.

History and Essence

An exorcism is commonly understood as an act of freeing someone from an evil spirit, often through incantations or ritual acts. Christians have a permanent memory of Jesus as one who cast out evil spirits. It is notable that Jesus exorcised unclean spirits without recourse to incantations or occult performances. Rather, he cast out demons by the Spirit of God (Matthew 12:28).[3] Jesus is remembered also as empowering all who believe in him—and not just a select few—to cast out demons (Mark 16:17). As Jesus united himself with the power of the Spirit through fasting and prayer, so did his followers understand that this ministry must be exercised in the context of a similar discipline (Mark 9:28; Matthew 17:20).

After the death and resurrection of Jesus, the early community continued to cast out demons in Jesus' name.[4] In mid–second century Rome, Justin Martyr (died about 165) testified to the existence of this ministry throughout Christianity.[5] In the following century, the African theologian Origen (died about 254) confirmed that Christians exorcised demons in the name of Jesus.[6] Although catechumens were not numbered among the possessed, the ancient church did believe that catechumens were particularly susceptible to the influence and power of darkness. Thus it was common to perform exorcisms over the catechumens. For example, the *Apostolic Tradition* of Hippolytus, written about 215, records that catechumens were prayed over after instructional sessions. This ritual act, which included the laying on of hands, usually is interpreted as an exorcism.[7] The "Procatechesis" of Cyril of Jerusalem, delivered around the year 360, contains an even clearer reference to catechumenal exorcisms.[8] Although Cyril does not mention exorcisms before the stage of purification and enlightenment, one safely can presume that such occurred.

Although the adult catechumenate disappeared in Western Christianity by the early Middle Ages,[9] texts for the major exorcisms of the elect survived in various forms in some liturgical books. The more informal and improvisatory rituals before election to Easter sacraments such as the minor exorcisms, however, virtually disappeared from the Christian repertory. With the reemergence of the adult catechumenate in this century, the major exorcisms again assumed a prominent place in this ritual process. The more improvisational and, therefore, amorphous series of rituals such as the minor exorcisms that punctuated the catechumenal process before election, however, have not so easily moved back into the mainstream of catechumenal rituals. One might suggest that these were restored more in theory than in practice.

Purpose and Frequency

The official introduction to the minor exorcisms suggests that their purpose is to "draw the attention of the catechumens to the real nature of Christian life, the struggle between flesh and spirit, the importance of self-denial for reaching the blessedness of God's kingdom and the unending need for God's help" (RCIA, 90). This analysis is confirmed by the 11 alternate prayer texts for the exorcisms contained in the rite. These prayers, which are the central element of the rite, are offered to God by the community for the catechumens. These prayers characteristically ask God to "protect them," "free them from evil," "strengthen them on their way" and "hold in check the power of the evil one." Such texts demonstrate that the minor exorcisms essentially are intercessory moments during which the community offers prayers for the candidates, particularly in view of the difficult process of conversion in faith.

These prayers are distinguished from the prayers of the major exorcisms (scrutinies) by a certain degree of intensity. The prayers of the minor exorcisms, for example, tend to be deprecatory in form, asking God for help on the journey toward conversion. The prayers of the major exorcisms, however, often employ a strong imperative. These usually are more forceful and succinct in their language and structure, asking God to free the elect from evil. A comparison of the second prayer for the minor exorcisms and the first prayer for the major exorcism during the third scrutiny illustrates this point:

Minor Exorcism

Lord our God,
you make known the true life;
you cut away corruption
and strengthen faith,
you build up hope and foster love.
In the name of your beloved Son,
our Lord Jesus Christ,
and in the power of the Holy Spirit,
we ask you to remove from these
        your servants,
all unbelief and hesitation in faith,
[the worship of false gods and magic,
witchcraft and dealings with the dead]
the love of money and lawless passions,
enmity and quarreling,
and every manner of evil.
And because you have called them
to be holy and sinless in your sight
create in them a spirit of faith
        and reverence,
of patience and hope,
of temperance and purity,
and of charity and peace.
We ask this through Christ our Lord.
Amen.

Major Exorcism

Father of life and God not of the dead
but of the living,
you sent your Son to proclaim life
to snatch us from the realm of death,
and to lead us to the resurrection.
Free these elect
from the death-dealing power of the
spirit of evil,
so that they may bear witness
to their new life in the risen Christ,
for he lives and reigns for ever
        and ever.
Amen.

One of the reasons that the prayers of the major exorcisms seem more forceful is that they always are followed by a second prayer that often is more consoling and deprecatory in the style of the minor exorcisms.[10] Furthermore, the dramatic and decisive nature of the period of purification and enlightenment naturally calls forth more dramatic and imperative prayer forms.

Though we might characterize the prayers of the minor exorcisms as gentler and more deprecatory than those of the major exorcisms, there are many differences in these texts that suggest their usage in different circumstances. Some of the prayers, such as the one quoted here, are more appropriate at the beginning of the catechumenal journey. This prayer is especially well suited to the ritual suggestion that a first exorcism and renunciation of false worship might be inserted into the rite of acceptance into the order of catechumens.[11] Prayer C has a similar beginning: In it the assembly asks God to "receive them into your kingdom and open their hearts to understand your gospel so that . . . they may become members of your church." Option F, however, suggests a later stage in the catechumenal journey as it prays, "Look kindly on the efforts and the progress of your servants. Strengthen them on their way, increase their faith and accept their repentance." Finally, option H implies that election is at hand: "We pray for these your servants who have opened their ears and hearts to your word. Grant that they may grasp your moment of grace." Not all of the prayers for the minor exorcisms have such specific references. Many do, however, and should be used sensitively in accordance with the varying moments of the catechumens' journey toward election.

These texts, as well as the official instruction,[12] presume that the minor exorcisms will be employed throughout the entire catechumenal process. The challenge is to use these exorcisms often enough so that the catechumens can experience their ritual import, while not using them so often that they become routine.

Two principles must be observed when meeting this challenge. First, numerous rituals are proper to the catechumenal journey: anointings, blessings, celebrations of the word, etc. The breadth of this repertory must be respected and explored. The presumption is that the more effective the ritual language of the entire catechumenate is, the more effective the minor exorcisms will be. Second, the minor exorcisms challenge catechumens by addressing the difficulties of conversion with strong penitential overtones. All exorcisms differ, for example, from anointings, which calm and soothe. This is especially true when an anointing is joined with an affirming blessing.[13] An exorcism, by contrast, emphasizes the more penitential elements of this ritual repertory.

Consequently, minor exorcisms, like anointings or blessings, cannot be scheduled as calendar dates in the catechumenal journey. Nor can one simply rotate exorcisms, anointings and blessings on a tripartite schedule after each meeting of catechumens. Rather, catechists and sponsors must monitor experiences of catechumens and shape appropriate rituals in view of such experiences. Especially in times of discernment, recognition of sin, personal struggle or even tension within the catechumenal community, minor exorcisms may be appropriate. Catechumens not elected for Easter sacraments might find exorcisms an effective lenten experience. Exorcisms also might be effective in conjunction with the church's ember days or during other periods of fasting and penance. Attention to the dynamics of exorcism will allow these rituals to occur with integrity.

Structure, Adaptation and Ministry

According to the ritual, minor exorcisms consist of a single prayer proclaimed by a celebrant with hands outstretched over the catechumens, who bow or kneel during the prayer (90–93). Accordingly,

> The minor exorcisms take place within a celebration of the word of God held in a church, a chapel or in a center for the catechumenate. A minor exorcism also may be held at the beginning or the end of a meeting for catechesis. When some special need exists, one of these prayers of exorcism may be said privately for individual catechumens.

It is assumed that minor exorcisms ordinarily are public events. The exorcism affirms that the catechumenal journey itself is a public event in the life of the church. As a sacramental process, the catechumenate is a fully ecclesial act that requires and challenges the faith commitment of the entire local community. It is the engagement of the local church that enables catechumens to journey with integrity toward their public incorporation into the Christian community at the Easter Vigil.

Ultimately, the ritual gives us little information on the enactment of these rites other than the prayer texts themselves, an indication of ministry, a very broad note on the time of the rituals and a reference to the extended hands of the presider over the bowing or kneeling catechumens. Aside from incidental comments about time, place and ministry, the ritual consists of one element: the prayer. Though the instruction does note that the minor exorcisms may take place within a liturgy of the word, even in this context it is an impoverished ritual unit. This ritual impoverishment seems to be addressed by the suggestion that minor exorcisms might take place with either the blessing of catechumens or the anointing.[14] Though combining these actions may strengthen their ritual impact, it may not always be the most appropriate solution. Rather than enriching or expanding an individual rite, this approach simply strings the actions together. The result is an indistinct amalgam of catechumenal gestures that could blur the meaning of each rite as well as blunt its effectiveness in various combinations.

The minor exorcisms are a valuable part of the catechumenal ritual repertory and must stand on their own. This means that the rites must be expanded and adapted, which could be accomplished in a number of ways. First, as in the blessings of the catechumens (97), it is possible and appropriate to lay hands on the catechumens individually after the prayer of exorcism. The rich symbolic horizons of this gesture certainly allow it to operate effectively in an exorcistic context. After the laying on of hands, it might be effective for the community to join together in the Lord's Prayer.[15] The penitential nature of this prayer, with its request for deliverance from evil and temptation, makes it a fitting climax to the rite. A simple dismissal such as "Go in peace— Thanks be to God" would follow.

In addition to expanding the rite *after* the central prayer of exorcism, it also is appropriate to *prepare* more deliberately for it. Music may serve to prepare the community for the rite: quiet instrumental music, a sung responsory, a simple litany or a mantra.[16] In general, the music should be subdued and, like the prayer itself, petitionary in nature. After simple, repetitive music, the catechumens may be invited to mention any special difficulty or weakness that they would like exorcised from their lives. This suggestion is offered in view of the overly passive role for catechumens in this and other catechumenal rites. If we expect catechumens to develop into active members of the church who stand up and profess their faith, then participation in the catechumenal rites should model this active role in the church. Catechumens are not mannequins on whom the church imposes its magic. They are adults on their journey toward full initiation in the church. The rite should, therefore, be an adult rite that encourages them to speak and act, not simply be spoken to or acted on.[17] Though they are not the main ministers in the rite, catechumens still have a ministry to each other as well as to the wider community. Giving them an active role in this rite affirms this ministry.

Though the prayer of exorcism is the central element, it is possible to configure supplementary ritual elements around that prayer to craft a fuller rite. One proposed ritual outline is as follows:

Opening litany/mantra/response

Introduction and invitation to catechumens to mention
    their needs in prayer

Silent prayer

Prayer of exorcism[18]

Laying on of hands

Our Father

Dismissal

Circumstances may exist when a minor exorcism is effectively celebrated privately with a catechumen. When confronting a particular or long-standing demon or at times of weakened spiritual fervor or personal failure, this rite can prove powerful. Devoid of the musical component, the simplified private rite might begin by asking the catechumen to pray for deliverance from the particular weakness or difficulty. Inviting the catechumen to kneel, the minister then recites the prayer of exorcism, followed by the laying on of hands, the Our Father and the sign of peace. This provides a rite that is substantive though not pretentious or preemptive of the major exorcisms or other rites of election.

Conclusion

A true spirit of mystagogy means trusting the rite. It means acknowledging that explanation does not supplant worship, that catechesis does not preempt praise. The journey toward full initiation is less a matter of mind than one of heart. It is precisely such catechumenal rites as the minor exorcisms that probe the heart and speak to it with unparalleled clarity. These ultimately are events of and in the spirit of Jesus. By respecting, adapting and enacting the minor exorcisms, we do more than revive an ancient tradition or enliven an important parochial program. Rather, we affirm that conversion is not contained by human intelligence but achieved through divine wisdom. The church teaches that, more than anywhere else, this divine wisdom becomes present to the community through its worship. By enacting the rites with integrity and imagination, we let the Spirit that brought the church into being guide those who long to be a part of that church.

Notes

[1] The rites of the catechumenal period comprise 45 pages (17–61) in the LTP edition of the *Rite of Christian Initiation of Adults*. This includes 20 pages on the rite of acceptance into the order of catechumens at the start of the catechumenate (17–36), one page on the optional presentations that normally take place during the period of enlightenment (55) and six pages on the last rite of the catechumenate, the optional sending of the catechumens for election (56–61). Thus, the actual rites for the period of the catechumenate encompass only 18 pages in the ritual (37–54), though this period might last for years. The rites for the elect, including initiation, however, comprise 78 pages (63–150).

[2] See RCIA, 79, 106–117.

[3] Isaac Mendelsohn, "Exorcism," *Interpreter's Dictionary of the Bible*, 2:199.

[4] In the Acts of the Apostles, for example, Paul casts out an evil spirit, saying, "In the name of Jesus Christ I command you, come out of her" (16:18).

5 "For numberless demoniacs throughout the whole world and in your city, many of our Christian men exorcising them in the name of Jesus Christ who was crucified under Pontius Pilate have healed and do heal, rendering helpless and driving the possessing devils out of men." Justin Martyr, *The Second Apology,* 5.2, translation from *The Ante-Nicene Fathers,* 1:190.

6 "A similar philosophy applies also to our Jesus, whose name already has been seen in an unmistakable manner to have expelled myriads of evil spirits from the souls and bodies [of men], so great was the power that it exerted upon those from whom the spirits were driven out." *Origen against Celsus,* 1:25, translation from *The Ante-Nicene Fathers,* 4:406.

7 "When the teacher has finished giving instruction, let the catechumens pray by themselves, separated from the faithful; and let the women, whether faithful or catechumens, stand by themselves in some place in the church when they pray. And when they have finished praying, they shall not give the Peace, for their kiss is not yet holy. But let only the faithful greet one another, men with men, and women with women; but the men shall not greet the women. And let all the women cover their heads with a hood, but [not] just with a piece of linen, for that is no veil. After their prayer, when the teacher has laid hands on the catechumens, he shall pray and dismiss them. Whether the teacher is a cleric or a layman, let him act thus." Hippolytus, *Apostolic Tradition,* chapters 18–19, trans. by Geoffrey J. Cuming, *Hippolytus: A Text for Students* (Bramcott Notts: Grove Books, 1976).

8 "Let thy feet hasten to the catechizing; receive with earnestness the exorcisms: whether thou be breathed upon or exorcised, the act is to thee salvation." Cyril of Jerusalem, *Procatechesis,* 9, translation from *Nicene and Post-Nicene Fathers of the Christian Church,* 2nd series, 7:3.

9 *Ordo Romanus* 11, which may have appeared between 650 and 700, indicates that the adult catechumenate no longer existed in Rome.

10 The prayer following the major exorcism cited here, for example, is "Lord Jesus Christ, you commanded Lazarus to step forth alive from his tomb and by your own resurrection freed all people from death. We pray for these your servants, who eagerly approach the waters of new birth and hunger for the banquet of life. Do not let the power of death hold them back, for, by their faith, they will share in the triumph of your resurrection, for you live and reign for ever and ever. Amen" (RCIA, 175).

[11] "The conference of bishops has discretionary power to make the following decision . . . to insert into the rite of acceptance into the order of catechumens a first exorcism and renunciation of false worship in regions where paganism is widespread [the NCCB has approved leaving to the discretion of the diocesan bishop this inclusion of a first exorcism and a renunciation of false worship in the rite of acceptance into the order of catechumens]" (RCIA, 33).

[12] "The formularies for the minor exorcisms may be used on several occasions, as different situations may suggest" (RCIA, 93).

[13] "The anointing may be followed by a blessing of the catechumens" (RCIA, 101).

[14] "Celebrations of the word that are held in connection with instructional sessions may include, along with an appropriate reading, a minor exorcism (94) or a blessing of the catechumens (97). When the minor exorcism is used, it may be followed by one of the blessings (97) or, on occasion, by the rite of anointing (102–103)" (Note on RCIA, 89).

[15] Each local community must decide whether the inclusion of the Lord's Prayer within this catechumenal rite would support or diminish the presentation of the Lord's Prayer (RCIA, 178–184) during the period of the catechumenate or the period of purification and enlightenment.

[16] A chanted "Kyrie eleison," Dan Schutte's "Send us your Spirit" and the Taizé "Miserere Nobis" or "Veni Sancte Spiritus" are examples of such music.

[17] The *Apostolic Tradition* of Hippolytus, for example, notes that the catechumens pray apart from the faithful before receiving the laying on of hands. See note 7.

[18] If one has employed a simple mantra for the opening, e.g. "Veni Sancte Spiritus," it is possible for the community to repeat this mantra quietly underneath the prayer of exorcism and during the laying on of hands.

4

BLESSINGS OF THE CATECHUMENS

Ever since the *Rite of Christian Initiation of Adults* was first promulgated in 1972, catechists, liturgists, musicians, priests and parish teams have spent considerable time and energy studying and learning to celebrate the many ritual elements of initiation. The major rites (acceptance into the order of catechumens, election and the Easter Vigil itself) have been the topics of many articles and workshops. Almost overlooked, however, have been the minor rites, such as anointings, minor exorcisms and blessings.

The *Rite of Christian Initiation of Adults,* 75.3, states that "the church . . . helps the catechumens on their journey by means of suitable liturgical rites which purify the catechumens little by little and strengthen them with God's blessing." This chapter will address the issue of blessings—when, how and by whom they are used—and how their use can enrich the catechumen's and candidate's experience.

"Blessing" refers both to praising and thanking God, and to requesting God's loving care for us. To bless is to acknowledge God's presence, to call down the protection of God on a person and to open that person up to God's love in and through the intercession of the community. To bless someone

MARGUERITE
MAIN

is to recognize their need—and ours—for God; we acknowledge that in this moment, in this person, in this community, God has been revealed to us, and we give thanks for that.

Blessings in Scripture

The Judeo-Christian heritage is rich in the tradition of blessings. In Genesis (1:22, 28), God blessed all living things with the power of generativity ("Be fertile and multiply"). God's words to Abraham, "I will make of you a great nation . . ." (Genesis 12:2–3), reflect that same blessing. In Hebrew tradition, certain individuals possessed special authority to call down God's blessings on others; for example, a father on his children (Genesis 49:25–26), a king on his subjects (2 Samuel 6:18) and priests on the people (Numbers 6:22–27). Blessing prayers were so prevalent among our Hebrew ancestors that the common verb for "to bless" *(berak)* also meant "to greet" or "to welcome"; apparently, our ancestors customarily welcomed others in God's name.

The invocation of the sacred name was made so that persons or the work of creation would be showered with divine blessings. Whether spoken by God or by others, God's blessing was always a promise of help and a reminder of the covenant God made with the people. It reflected a sense of dependence on the Lord as the source of all good things. By praising and blessing God, the Israelites solemnly acknowledged God as the Lord and King from whom all blessings flowed.

One of the most beautiful examples of blessing in the Christian Scriptures is found in Mark 10:13–16, which shows Jesus welcoming little children, putting his arms around them and blessing them. There are many other occasions in the gospels where Jesus blesses his disciples, blesses and praises God, blesses food before it is eaten. In Luke's gospel, Jesus blesses the disciples prior to his ascension; the disciples then return to Jerusalem blessing and praising God (Luke 24:50–53). Here the two aspects of blessing are manifest: the calling down of God's bounty on us, and thanksgiving and praise rendered back to God.

Blessings in the Life of the Church

Next to the sacraments themselves, the chief sacramental actions of the church always have been blessings. Since the Second Vatican Council, a tremendous renewal has taken place in the church. Prayer has been at the heart of that renewal, and nowhere is that more evident than in the blessings and prayers that express the way of life of all the faithful. *Catholic Household Blessings and Prayers,* published by the National Conference of Catholic Bishops, contains prayers that reflect the faith of countless generations of Christians who marked the days and nights, births and deaths, the large and the small joys and sorrows of life.

As sacramentals, blessings are "sacred signs that dispose us for the grace of the sacraments and render holy various occasions in life" *(Catholic Encyclopedia).* They call attention to God's presence and help to mark important times in one's life. They have both spiritual and temporal benefits, providing strength as needed to handle difficult times, or perhaps easing the pain of sorrow. By helping to proclaim the good news of God's love, they may enrich one's faith life as the Spirit of God is encountered in word and action.

Blessings in Contemporary Society

In our high-tech world, where everything seems to demand a scientific explanation, and where we seek practical solutions for every problem, returning to the practice of giving blessings or calling on God to enter our lives may require some effort. Perhaps we have forgotten how blessed our lives are and how we have experienced God's blessing. How ready are we to look at ourselves and at all of creation as being blessed by God? Perhaps we have become so attuned to the voices that proclaim the values of individualism, of doing things "my way," of the self-made man or woman, that we have lost the ability to recognize the unearned blessings of life given to us by our Creator. Perhaps in our technologically oriented world, where everything has a scientific reason for being, we have forgotten how to walk in awe and mystery and how to give thanks for the magnificence of creation. In a world where self-sufficiency is praised and independence is valued, perhaps we have lost the ability to stand naked before God and acknowledge our dependency. Perhaps we have forgotten what it means to bless and be blessed.

David Haas has written a song often used at the celebration of the rite of election. The words of the acclamation in that song are "Blessed be God, who calls you by name, holy and chosen one" (*Who Calls You by Name,* Chicago: GIA Publications, 1988). How ready are we to believe that we really are holy and chosen ones? Just as we have to learn what it means to be a welcoming community before we can provide a properly welcoming ceremony for the rite of acceptance, perhaps we also need to be reminded that we are indeed "holy and chosen ones" before we can effectively use the blessings provided in the *Rite of Christian Initiation of Adults.*

The Blessing of Catechumens

The rite (97) offers nine blessings for catechumens. These blessings are an extension of the church's liturgical action to those who are preparing for baptism. They are bestowed on the catechumens "so that even though they do not as yet have the grace of the sacraments, they may still receive from the church courage, joy and peace as they proceed along the difficult journey they have begun" (RCIA, 95). They are strong, visible signs of the care and concern of the church, and of God's love for the catechumens.

When To Bless   There are many occasions during the catechumen-ate when it is not only appropriate but also effective to use one of the prayers of blessing. Though usually used at the end of a celebration of the word, they also may be used as a dismissal blessing or as a closing prayer for a catechetical session with the catechumens. In addition, a blessing also may be used with individuals or with a group whenever there is some particular reason to do so. For example, a catechetical session may have exposed an area of great pain or struggle in a person's life. There may have been a real conversion experience, a time when the mysteries of death and resurrection have been met head on, a moment when the truth of God's word has broken through and become real or a time when one is deeply in need of the healing power of God's love. The nine options offered in the rite speak to these needs and may be adapted, if necessary, to apply to the particular situation.

Adaptations Although the rite specifically refers to the use of the blessings for catechumens, adaptation can make their use appropriate for both catechumens and candidates for full communion. Candidates, too, struggle with issues of conversion, of temptation and sin, of death and resurrection. Although they are one with us in baptism, they are not yet fully in union with us sacramentally. The grace of these blessings answers a need in both candidates and catechumens.

The *Rite of Christian Initiation of Adults* (35) encourages adaptation of the rites where necessary to fit the circumstances or special situation of the catechumens and candidates. The models given are necessarily general. Adaptation, however, does not mean change for the sake of change. It does mean being sensitive both to the structure and meaning of the ritual itself and to the circumstances or special needs of the group, and then working within the confines of the ritual to provide a text that will accommodate both.

Structure Before attempting to adapt any of the blessings offered in the rite, the catechist or other presider must be familiar with the elements of a prayer of blessing. Ritual prayer is not made up out of whole cloth, but rather it draws on the tradition and contains certain patterns identifiable to the participants.

The blessing prayer itself generally follows the collect format ("you–who–do–through"):

1. Naming of God ("you"): not a name selected arbitrarily but one chosen in relation to the particular circumstances or relating to the scripture reading ("God of comfort and mercy . . .");

2. An expansion of the address of God ("who"), calling to mind what God has done in the past, or praising God;

3. Petitions for God's help ("do") asking for God's blessing on the catechumens at this particular moment, calling on God to listen, to come to their assistance;

4. The conclusion of the prayer ("through"), which reaffirms the belief that our prayer begins and ends in Jesus Christ, who intercedes in our behalf ("We ask this through Christ our Lord . . .").

Blessings derive their meaning and effectiveness from God's word, and therefore scripture always should be an integral part of any blessing liturgy. If the blessing is not incorporated into a celebration of the word or a session of lectionary-based catechesis, an appropriate scripture reading should be provided. A typical blessing ritual might consist of:

Gathering and call to prayer

Sign of the cross

Introductory comments by presider (as necessary)

Reading of scripture

Silence or brief reflection on the word

Prayer of blessing

Conclusion (sign of the cross or word of dismissal)

Prayers of intercession may also be offered after the reading of the word, prior to the blessing. A song may be sung at the beginning and/or at the end of the prayer, and a familiar psalm could be sung after the reading.

Ministers Blessings may be given, according to the rite (96), by a priest, a deacon or a designated catechist. The relationship that has developed between the catechist and the catechumens and candidates makes it especially fitting that the catechist might be the one to give these blessings. Paragraph 16 in the rite states that whenever possible catechists should play an active part in the rites, and the blessings are an appropriate place for that to happen.

The leader of the prayer, whether catechist, deacon or priest, will be effective only to the extent that he or she is a person of prayer and is in touch with the need and longing for God that is in each of us. The leader should be able to lend dignity to the prayer by being comfortable in the role. This means the leader must become familiar with the ritual, understanding the various elements (prayer, song, scriptures, silence, gestures) and how they interact in this service.

Gestures and Symbols Gestures and symbols are important in the Jewish and Christian prayer traditions. When carried out with dignity and in a spirit of faith, they may help to deepen the meaning for all who participate. Some appropriate gestures and symbols that might be incorporated into a prayer of blessing include:

The sign of the cross:
> May be made over all the participants.
> May be made individually over the person(s) being blessed.
> May be traced by the presider on the foreheads of participants.
> May be made in unison by the entire group.

Use of hands:
> Presider may extend his or her hands toward or over those being blessed.
> Presider may impose hands on the participants (especially meaningful in times of pain and healing).
> Presider may pray with hands folded or upraised.

Holy water:
> Holy water may be sprinkled or individuals may bless themselves with it. (This is especially appropriate for baptized candidates.)

Incense:
> Incense is a symbol of purification and prayer, and its use may add solemnity to the moment.

Silence:
> Silence is always an appropriate and effective part of prayer. All too often we feel that we must fill every moment with words. A time of silence, with or without a gesture such as laying on of hands, offers a time for the words of the blessing and the proclaimed Word to fill the heart and mind of the catechumen.

In multicultural parishes, some elements of the blessing may be given in different languages, according to the identity of the group. There also may be a particular gesture or symbol that would reflect a specific ethnic tradition and would help express the meaning of the rite to that particular group. I recently attended a multicultural consultation in Seattle sponsored by the North American Forum on the Catechumenate. One morning, prayer was led by a Native American woman using a traditional purification or blessing rite of her people. This blessing, called a "smudging," is used in a group setting to purify the mind and to center oneself prior to prayer, to hearing the Word, or even prior to Mass. The sacred smoke from burning grasses, cedar or sage, represents the Great Spirit or Creator God. Participants sit in a circle around the smudge pot as a sign that they are all equal before their God. The smoke is passed to each individual to allow them to bless themselves with it. It was a powerful yet simple action. I could not help but be moved by the realization that a people who always have had a rich tradition of ritual and blessing had incorporated this sign as a part of their Christian prayer. How welcoming it would be to include traditional rituals of the ethnic groups in our parishes into our prayers and blessings!

Blessings are a rich part of the liturgical life of our church. They can be used very effectively to enrich the experience of the catechumenate as a source of "food for the journey" for the catechumens and candidates, and to make holy the various situations in life in which they find themselves. We, as catechists, priests and team members, to be effective in imparting these blessings, *must* take time to get in touch with our own need for God so that we also might live as "holy and chosen ones."

5

SENDING OF THE CATECHUMENS FOR ELECTION

Have you ever noticed, while working with the ritual text for Christian initiation, the small notations in the right-hand margin? Have you wondered to what these numbers and "USA" refer? A number refers to a particular paragraph's number in the 1974 provisional translation of the text by the International Commission on English in the Liturgy (ICEL). The indication "USA" identifies those paragraphs or sections of the rite that were created by and for the church in the United States. Their inclusion in the official ritual text indicates that, although not a part of the universal text, they have been confirmed by Rome. The rite of sending of the catechumens for election is a prime example of what is called a "conference-specific inclusion," thus the notation "USA" alongside the title of this rite.

In commenting on the rite of sending, I will focus on four points—history, structure, meaning, and pastoral considerations—following the structure of Michel Dujarier in his book *The Rites of Christian Initiation* (New York: Wm. H. Sadlier, Inc., 1979). This was a critical text for my own understanding of the rites of Christian initiation. After commenting on the rite of sending of the catechumens for election, I will include some

RONALD

A.

OAKHAM

comments on the rite of sending the candidates for recognition by the bishop and for the call to continuing conversion.

Historical Overview

The rite of sending came into being when dioceses began to prepare celebrations of the rite of election. The ritual presumes, although it does not explicitly state, that the rite of election will be a diocesan celebration. The introductory notes for this rite indicate that it is presided over by the bishop or his delegate (RCIA, 121); that it is cele-brated on the First Sunday of Lent, but for "urgent pastoral reasons it is permitted to celebrate the rite of election during the week preceding or following the First Sunday of Lent" (125); and that the proper place for its celebration is the cathedral church, but allow for a parish church or other "suitable and fitting place" (127) to be used. The "bottom line" is that this celebration is removed from the parish setting.

When the implementation of the order of Christian initiation of adults was in its early stages, many pastoral ministers were concerned about this step in the journey being removed from the experience of the parish community. The transition from the catechumenate period to the period of purification and enlightenment thus would occur unbe-knownst to the community. In response to this concern, several pastoral practices emerged.

In some parishes, the remedy was to ignore the diocesan rite and celebrate election on their own, often without seeking delegation from the bishop. This solution betrays a congregational sense of church, which is not true to our tradition.

Some dioceses decided not to plan a diocesan celebration until the parish communities had experienced a rite of election for several years. In these situations, pastors who wished to celebrate election were instructed to write to the bishop indicating that they had catechumens who were ready for the sacraments of initiation and requesting appropriate delegation. In response, the bishop would send a letter of delegation that included some comments addressed to the catechumens, which was to be read as a part of the parish celebration. This practice recognized that the parish is a part of a larger, universal body and avoided the congregationalism of the first practice described. It is, however, a minimal symbol.

A third response was the development of a rite of sending. It was developed by the archdiocese of Chicago in 1979 and the diocese of Brooklyn in 1983 working independently of each other. Ron Lewinski wrote about the Chicago experience in the archdiocesan newsletter for catechumenate ministers, *Chicago Catechumenate,* predecessor of *Catechumenate: A Journal of Christian Initiation* published by Liturgy Training Publications.

In both dioceses, this pastoral response was based on a rubric in the 1974 provisional translation (146) that indicated that if there were a great number of catechumens, "a list of names may be given to the celebrant." The diocesan leaders' presumed that the catechumens would have signed their names at an earlier gathering. Rather than simply having this done as an afterthought at the end of some catechumenate gathering, these leaders designed a parish ritual to prepare for the rite of election, which would be celebrated as a diocesan event.

As word spread around the country about these adapted rites, many dioceses began to offer this adaptation. Because of the widespread satisfaction with this adaptation, one form of it was included in the proposed revisions of the *Rite of Christian Initiation of Adults.* It received approval by the United States bishops and was confirmed by the Congregation for Divine Worship. Thus it exists within the main body of the ritual text as a rite belonging to the catechumenate period. It is designated as "optional" because it is not a required celebration, but a pastoral offering.

The Meaning of This Rite

The rite of sending stands in the shadow of the rite of election. Thus, to understand the meaning of the sending, we must first understand the meaning of election.

The rite of election ritualizes two facets of the initiation journey: the initiative of God in the lives of the catechumens and the catechumens' response to God.

The initiative of God is to call a person to God's self, to invite the other into relationship. Our tradition speaks of those who are so invited by God as the "elect," those on whom God's favor rests. It is the church's responsibility to discern this action of God in the lives of the catechumens. If we can identify the presence of God reflected in their lives, we can declare with confidence that they are truly God's chosen ones. This declaration is made by the bishop in the part of the celebration called "act of admission or election." In this act, the church gives voice to the call of God.

The catechumens, for their part, are to give evidence of their response to God's initiative by declaring their intent to celebrate the Easter sacraments. This declaration is done in two ways: by verbally answering the bishop's inquiry regarding their desire to celebrate the Easter sacraments and by inscribing their names in the book of the elect (cf. RCIA, 132).

Enrollment of Names   Signing a book as a part of this rite is a recent inclusion. Although there are historical accounts of bishops gathering the names of those who are ready for the Easter sacraments, there is no record of the catechumens signing a book of the elect. This signing is a modern attempt to include some ritual action in a very verbal rite. As a new symbolic action, its meaning is still unfolding.

The ritual text indicates that "this step is also called the enrollment of names because as a pledge of fidelity the candidates inscribe their names in the book that lists those who have been chosen for initiation" (119). By this act, the candidates for election indicate that any questions or decisions that would keep them from celebrating the sacraments at the next Easter have been resolved. In effect, they are "putting their nickel down," surrendering themselves to Christ and to his church.

But as we experience this act of inscribing, our understanding of it takes on different nuances. Many people see in this symbol an image of what the scriptures call the book of life (cf. Revelation 21: 27).

Although this image of the book of the elect does not seem to have been intended by the writers of the ritual, it has been given credence with the 1988 revised rite. This edition includes sample adapted rites for baptized, uncatechized candidates seeking full communion with the Catholic Church. In the rite that corresponds to the rite of sending, the rite of calling the candidates to continuing conversion (450–458), the candidates do not sign the book of the elect. This action has been omitted deliberately. The omission is based on the theology that the baptized candidates are already listed among the elect by virtue of their baptism. This reasoning fosters the idea that inscribing one's name at election is an image of one's name being entered into the book of life.

It should be noted that the decision to omit the signing by the candidates was not unanimous. Some members of the committee held that this action is the handing over of one's self to the community. As such, even baptized candidates should sign the book as they surrender themselves to the Catholic community. It is fair to say that the last word regarding this issue is not yet in.

Discernment of Readiness The text of the ritual is very clear that the church wants "to exclude any semblance of mere formality from the rite" (122) and therefore "there should be a deliberation prior to its celebration to decide on the catechumens' suitableness" (122). Thus, a discernment process that includes priests, deacons, catechists, godparents, representatives of the community, and the other catechumens is to be carried out. The outcome of this discernment is presented during the rite of election: "During the celebration of election, the assembly is informed of the decision approving the catechumens" (122).

The rite of sending also presumes that some deliberation has gone on prior to its celebration. It provides the "local community the opportunity to express its approval of the catechumens and to send them forth to the celebration of election assured of the parish's care and support" (107). Members of the community may speak publicly about those catechumens who have presented themselves for admission to the Easter sacraments. After those who will speak on the catechumens' behalf have done so, the assembly is invited to ratify what they have heard. In giving their assent, they are adding their testimony to that of those who know the catechumens personally. Having gathered all this testimony, the presider then sends the catechumens to the bishop with the recommendation of the parish community.

When the assembly that gathers at the rite of election "is informed of the decision approving the catechumens" (122), it will be not be the decision just of the "initiation ministers," but of the entire community. The ecclesial dimension of this rite is enhanced by the symbol of the church giving public testimony on behalf of the catechumens.

Structure of the Rite

The structure of the rite of sending is very simple, and quite similar to the rite of election. "The rite takes place after the homily in a celebration of the word of God or at Mass" (109). It begins with a presentation of the catechumens by a member of the parish: "the priest in charge of the catechumens' initiation, a deacon, a catechist or a representative of the community" (111). Included in this presentation is a brief introduction of what the catechumens are seeking.

In response to the presentation, the presider invites the catechumens to come forward along with their godparents. Once they have moved to a designated place, the presider asks for the testimony of the godparents. Three ritual questions are provided in the text. Following the godparents' testimony, the presider may ask the entire assembly for its approval of the catechumens. No specific text is given for this.

Having heard the testimonies (and received the assembly's assent), the presider declares the community's recommendation of the catechumens to the bishop. A rubric indicates that "if the signed book of the elect is to be presented to the bishop in the rite of election" (113), the catechumens may sign it as a part of this celebration, or at some time prior to the rite of election. The godparents "may also write their names along with the catechumens in the book of the elect" (123).

The community then prays for the catechumens with a series of intercessions that concludes with the presider praying with hands outstretched over the catechumens.

If the rite is celebrated within Mass, the catechumens are dismissed at this point. If it is a celebration of the word of God, the entire assembly is dismissed, and an appropriate song may be sung to conclude the celebration.

Except for the optional signing of the book of the elect, all the action of this rite of sending is that of the community on behalf of the catechumen, adding a ritual dimension to the deliberation on the catechumens' readiness (cf. 122), which is required for the authentic celebration of the rite of election.

Pastoral Considerations

Several pastoral issues and decisions regarding the rite of sending present themselves for consideration, ranging from the decision whether to celebrate the rite or not, to decisions regarding the details of the rite.

To Celebrate or Not To Celebrate   The first pastoral consideration regarding the rite of sending is whether or not it will be used in your parish. The most cogent reason for celebrating it, in my opinion, is that doing so enhances the ecclesial dimension of the step from the period of the catechumenate to the period of purification and enlightenment.

I have observed that most parishes that have implemented the process of adult initiation do celebrate the rite of sending. People's appreciation of it varies according to several factors, such as how it is celebrated and how much the catechumens have become a part of the community's life during the period of the catechumenate.

When a parish chooses not to celebrate this rite, the reason most often given is that the rite of election will take in that parish's church (either the cathedral or another designated church). Two factors influence this decision. The first is that the rite indicates: "When election will take place in the parish, this rite is not used" (106). This directive refers to situations in which the celebration of election will not be a diocesan event, but a parish event (with proper delegation, of course). But when it is a diocesan event that will be occurring in a parish church, it is not taking place "in the parish." In all likelihood, parishioners will not be present as a parish community. People of the parish who will participate in the rite will be present as representatives of this community within the context of the diocesan church.

The second factor is the rationale that since the catechumens are not going to another place, there is no reason for a rite of sending. The problem with this line of thinking is that it is not the place to which they are being sent, but the person. The catechumens are being sent to the bishop, not to the site of the rite of election. It is appropriate, therefore, for a parish that is hosting the rite of election in its church to celebrate a sending.

A second common reason offered for not celebrating this rite is that it "duplicates" election. This reasoning stems from a lack of understanding of the meaning of this rite in relationship to the rite of election. For those who have celebrated both the rites of sending and election, the distinction is clear. They often speak of how the diocesan celebration brought to completion the parish celebration.

The third most common reason is that it is too wordy and only encumbers the Sunday liturgy. True, it is a wordy ritual. Much creativity is required, therefore, to offset this reality. Attention to how the testimony is given and to the inclusion of the assembly in the action are key.

Time and Place　　The issue of encumbering the Sunday liturgy leads to another important consideration: the time and place for celebrating this rite. Most parishes celebrate it within the Sunday Mass on the First Sunday of Lent (following the pattern set by the rite of election). There is no directive in the rite, however, that says it should be celebrated then. The rite indicates only that it should be celebrated "at a suitable time prior to the rite of election" (108), "in a celebration of the word of God or at Mass" (109). The rite does presume the presence of many people from the community, and so many parishes schedule it at a time when such will be the case: Sunday Mass. This, however, may not be the best solution; what is already a stilted rite may be rendered even more lifeless to save time.

What is the alternative? Will a good representation of the community come to a special celebration during the week prior to the First Sunday of Lent? If the catechumenate period has been done well, the catechumens will have been involved in parish life. Many parishioners will know the catechumens personally and, when invited directly (not just by general invitation), are likely to participate. This, then, would allow for a more creative celebration than might be possible on a Sunday morning.

Ministers of the Rite   Who is the presider of the rite of sending? If the rite is celebrated at Sunday Mass, the priest who presides at the Sunday assembly obviously would preside over the sending. If, however, the rite of sending takes place within a celebration of the word of God, it is an open question. The rite is not specific about whether the presider is a priest, a deacon or a catechist. The only indication that the rite presumes the presider is a priest is in the presentation of the catechumens (111). It begins, "Reverend Father." More important than the presumption that a priest presides is the presumption that a designated leader of the parish presides. (It is the parish community's recommendation that is being gathered.) Thus, if a parish has a pastoral administrator and not a pastor, the administrator may very well preside at this rite.

The first action of the rite is the presentation of the catechumens. The most appropriate person to do this is the catechumenate director. A part of this person's role is to be the liaison between the catechumenal community and the parish community. The presenter should address both the presider and the assembly, indicating what the catechumens seek from them.

Placement of Catechumens and Godparents   The person who presents the catechumens may also invite them to come forward or to take their places along with their godparents. The rubric for placement of the catechumens indicates that they and their godparents "come forward and stand before the celebrant" (111). This often results in the group standing with their backs to the community. The non-verbal message is, "Assembly, you are not a part of this conversation between the catechumens, godparents and presider." Instead, arrange the catechumens and godparents in a way that is inclusive of the assembly. They might, for example, stand together in several places within the assembly, or they could move to the front of the church and stand facing the assembly, with the presider facing them from the midst of the assembly.

Decisions about placement must take into consideration audibility of the testimonies. If a microphone is needed, will those testifying have to be standing near a stationary microphone, or does the community have a movable microphone?

The presider's first action is to greet the catechumens, address members of the assembly about their responsibility at this point in the catechumens' journey, and request the testimony.

Sponsors or Godparents? Before looking at the testimony to be given, I want to address the issue of who accompanies the catechumen during this rite. The text indicates that it is the godparent, based on the fact that the godparents begin their ministry at the rite of election. The rite of sending is, however, one of the "Rites Belonging to the Catechumenate Period" (81–117). It takes place during the time when the ministry of sponsor is still active. It is appropriate, therefore, for the sponsor to give the testimony during the rite of sending, with the godparent testifying at the rite of election. If the sponsor will be the godparent also, this is a moot issue. If, however, the godparent is someone other than the sponsor, another question must be considered: How can we provide a fitting conclusion to the sponsor's ministry? Inviting the sponsor give the testimony during the rite of sending is one way of formally ending the sponsor's ministry. The sponsor speaks on the catechumen's behalf and entrusts him or her to the godparent, whose ministry begins at the rite of election.

The Testimony After the question of who will testify is resolved, the format of the testimony must be considered. The ritual text provides a question-and-answer format involving the presider and the godparent or sponsor (112). The suggested questions focus more on what the catechumen has done than on what God is doing. The result may be that those who testify (and the assembly present) will conclude that one must earn sacramental life. Such an understanding verges on Pelagianism, a heresy that held that each person achieves salvation with his or her own power. If the question and answer format is to be used, therefore, the presider, following the rubric that allows using "similar words," should develop questions that reflect more accurately the discernment of God's initiative in the catechumen's life.

One can also interpret "in similar words" as allowing the godparents or sponsors to give testimony in their own words. If this format is followed, the catechumenate coordinator or other team member should assist godparents (or sponsors) as they prepare their testimony, lest they present speeches suitable to a testimonial dinner rather than attestations to the work of God in the catechumens' lives.

To avoid relegating the assembly to a passive role, an acclamation that praises God could be sung after each testimony. After all the godparents or sponsors have spoken, the presider could invite members of the assembly to give testimony. After an appropriate time, the presider then would address the entire assembly, stating that those who know the catechumens believe they are ready to take the next step in their initiation. The presider would then ask if the community agrees with this judgment. The assembly can respond verbally or with applause; the presider then makes a statement of recommendation, and the acclamation of praise can be sung to draw this part of the rite to a close.

Signing the Book of the Elect   If the book of the elect is to be signed, this is best done after the testimony. Because the signing is merely a preparation of the book for presentation at the rite of election, the signing should be done simply. If the book is not already in place, it may be brought forward and placed on a writing table. (The altar is not a writing desk; the book should not rest on it. Nor should the book be held on the knees of a seated presider: This signing is not a commitment to a religious leader, as are the signings that take place in the profession ceremonies of religious communities). The book should be positioned in such a way that the assembly can see the act of inscribing the names. Singing or instrumental music can accompany this action. After each catechumen has signed the book, it can be given to the catechumenate director with a simple instruction to bring it to the bishop.

Intercessions for the Catechumens   The intercessions for the catechumens, although in the same form as the prayers of the faithful, are not general intercessions but specific prayers for the catechumens. It would be good to pray them in a way that would set them off from the usual general intercessions. For example, a sung response could be introduced, the intercessions could be spoken over instrumental music and the response sung after each intercession.

Blessing and Dismissal   The prayer preceding the dismissal is not a conclusion to the intercessions, such as that at the end of the prayer of the faithful. It is, rather, a separate prayer over the catechumens, a blessing; compare the texts for this prayer (115) with the texts of the blessings of the catechumens (97). Because it is the prayer of the whole assembly, all may be invited to extend their hands over the catechumens while the presider prays aloud.

When dismissing the catechumens, the presider may include a comment about sending them to the bishop for election.

Rite of Sending the Candidates for Recognition by the Bishop

If we understand the meaning and purpose of the rite of sending catechumens for election, the rite of sending the candidates for recognition by the bishop and for the call to continuing conversion (434–445) is easy to understand.

This rite provides the local community with "the opportunity to express its joy in the candidates' decision [to complete their initiation or be received into the full communion of the Catholic Church] and to send them forth to the celebration of recognition assured of the parish's care and support" (435). It is a simple, public affirmation of the candidates' growth in faith. The parish recognizes the candidates' renewed commitment to their baptismal relationship with Christ and his church, and sends them to the bishop that he might exhort them to "live in deeper conformity to the life of Christ" (441).

Affirming a person's growth in faith, and letting that person know of our support and concern is a very good thing to do. Many catechumenate leaders are unhappy with this rite, however, because it seems to relegate the baptized candidate to a "second-class-citizen" position. Consequently, many ministers adapt this rite by including testimony similar to that called for in the rite of sending for election, and by inviting the candidates to sign a "scroll of commitment."

This is, in my opinion, an unfortunate decision. The desire to ensure that the candidates feel included in the rites of sending is appropriate. But rather than attempt to treat them the same as the catechumens, we must help them recognize that they are a part of the rite of sending for election by virtue of their position among the baptized. As the candidates have journeyed with the catechumens throughout the catechumenal process, the candidates have had the opportunity to get to know the catechumens. When the assembly (i.e., the baptized community) is invited to give testimony, the candidates probably could speak well on their behalf. The candidates may also join in the prayers for and over the catechumens. It must be remembered that the candidates are one with us in baptism and so can rightfully help to prepare the catechumens for baptism.

After the community has focused on the catechumens, it is good to call attention to the fact that it is not only the catechumens who have been on a journey of faith, but also some who are already one with us in baptism. The rite of sending the candidates for recognition can then take place with appropriate simplicity.

Conclusion

The rites of sending are preparations for the rite of election, which marks the transition from the catechumenate period into the period of purification and enlightenment. The rites of sending are not a rite of election. In preparing and celebrating the rites of sending, every effort must be made to keep this distinction clear.

Election itself is a prebaptismal rite. It marks the beginning of the catechumens' period of final preparation for the waters of baptism, the anointing of confirmation and the eucharistic meal. The posture of the baptized during Lent is to stand in solidarity with the catechumens during their period of "more intense spiritual preparation" (139). In so doing, the baptized are prepared for a renewal of their own baptismal commitment during the great Easter Vigil. For the baptized, this will be expressed in the annual renewal of baptismal promises. Some of the baptized also will profess the Catholic faith for the first time, receive the anointing with chrism, and share at the eucharistic table for the first time.

The Roman liturgy is very clear that during this period, two groups are journeying together to the Easter Triduum: catechumens (those unbaptized) and Christians (those baptized). As initiation ministers we do our ministry best when we work to assure that what is clear in design is kept clear in practice.

If baptized Christians seeking full communion are feeling left out in Lent, the solution is not to adapt the rites in such a way that makes the candidates more at one with the catechumens; it is, rather to include in their formation experiences that will help them to recognize their oneness with the Catholic community in baptism.

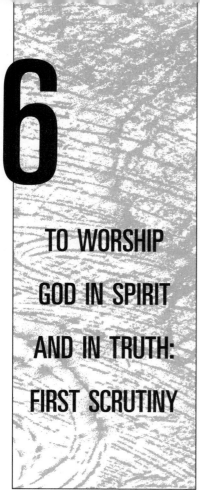

6

TO WORSHIP GOD IN SPIRIT AND IN TRUTH: FIRST SCRUTINY

Of the many strange sounding names proposed for celebrations by the *Rite of Christian Initiation of Adults,* perhaps none strikes ministers new to the process as more out of touch and archaic than "scrutiny." To those who speak modern English, a "scrutiny" celebrated during the period of "purification and enlightenment" sounds about as inviting as a trip to the dentist. Most people understand the verb "to scrutinize" as investigating or looking closely to see something that is not readily apparent, or to ferret out something less than desirable.

When the word *scrutiny* describes a liturgical celebration for the elect, it seems to imply a kind of heavenly interrogation to evaluate the honesty of the conversion claimed by those who have requested the sacraments of initiation. When the usual explanation of the scrutinies as "exorcisms" is used, the discomfort level of many people rises even higher, because they associate an exorcism with the special effects Hollywood employs to dramatize demonic possession.

It is unfortunate that these words conjure up popular associations that distort the intent and importance of these celebrations. But the very strangeness of the terms also invites the open-minded to delve more deeply into the purpose and

MARK R. FRANCIS

dynamism of the rites they describe. How did the early church understand these celebrations and why were they restored by the RCIA? Why are the scrutinies celebrated *for* the elect *by* the parish community? What is the particular thrust of the first scrutiny? What should be done with the already baptized candidates for full communion who are not to be scrutinized with the elect? The following reflections will address these questions and offer suggestions as to how the first scrutiny might be ritualized.

What Is a Scrutiny?

Early liturgical sources indicate that the scrutinies were not liturgical inquiries or interrogations made to ascertain the sincerity of the elect's conversion. Rather, these celebrations were solemn public intercessions made by the community of the faithful on behalf of those who already were chosen to receive the Easter sacraments. The form in which this prayer for their protection and deliverance was traditionally cast was that of an exorcism.

Because modern people associate exorcisms with horror movies, we often find it difficult to understand an exorcism's real purpose and emphasis. While many of the ancient prebaptismal exorcisms address Satan, they do so in a fashion that serves to emphasize the faith of the church in the power of Christ over evil. These exorcisms also stress that God already has called the elect to salvation through their approaching baptism. An ancient example of this kind of dramatic prayer is found in the *Old Gelasian Sacramentary,* one of the earliest sacramentaries of the Roman Rite.

> Therefore, accursed devil, recognize your condemnation and give honor to the living and true God; give honor, too, to Jesus Christ his Son and to the Holy Spirit; and keep far away from these servants of God; because God, our Lord Jesus Christ has deigned to call them to himself, to his holy grace and blessing, and to the font, the gift of baptism.[1]

Even though the devil is addressed, the emphasis of this traditional scrutiny exorcism is on God's might and protection, and on the call of the elect to baptism, not on the power of the devil. In much the same vein, centuries earlier, St. Paul named malevolent spirits in Romans 8:38 but proclaimed their powerlessness to separate Christians from God's all-conquering love in Jesus Christ. Clearly, the ancient church had a lively belief in the activity of evil spirits that influenced human life. Those who had not yet renounced Satan and his demons at baptism still were considered vulnerable to diabolical influences and in need of the powerful intercessory prayer offered by the assembly of baptized Christians.[2]

The Scrutinies and Christian Initiation

While both the word *scrutiny* and the worldview that produced it may seem to have little to do with modern life, the human confrontation with evil they describe still takes place every day. We modern folks might not personify our demons the way the early Christians did, but the presence of evil in our world certainly is not something that we can relegate to the distant past. A brief perusal of the newspaper on any morning reveals the extent to which the world turns its back on the redeeming love of God. Wars, genocide, greed, racial bigotry, religious intolerance and sexual violence all figure prominently in our news reports. Their presence in the world testifies that the human race, despite great technological advances, has progressed very little in the ways of God over the centuries. The demons that afflict our society might not be personalized by us, but they still exercise a powerful hold over many minds and hearts. Our contemporaries cry out for liberation from these and all powers that individually and collectively oppress and enslave human life.

Catholics both plead for and celebrate liberation from these evils in the scrutinies. Through these prayers, we acknowledge God's power to free us from that which makes us less than human, from that which separates us from God's love. Just as the ancient exorcisms did not concentrate on the power of the demon, so the modern scrutinies and their exorcisms—far from pointing an accusatory finger at the elect, whose weakness and guilt often remind us of our own—confidently proclaim God's power to help us overcome these evils. James Dunning describes an essential element to exorcism and scrutiny: "We do not exorcise to reveal our guilt but to reveal our poverty—our absolute dependence on God for healing. Only those can be liberated who *know* they are enslaved."[3] As the introductory paragraphs of the RCIA point out, the scrutinies are celebrated precisely to promote an awareness of those sins from which the elect need to be freed. It is in this sense that the rite speaks of the purpose of the scrutinies "to inspire in the elect a desire for purification and redemption by Christ" and "to instruct them gradually about the mystery of sin, from which the whole world and every person longs to be delivered" (RCIA, 143).

The Two Parts of the Scrutiny

In re-proposing the scrutinies, the *Rite of Christian Initiation of Adults* emphasizes the need for the self-knowledge that can come only after meditation on God's word. For this reason, the scrutinies take place after the proclamation of the word and the homily. The celebration begins with petitions inspired by the gospel, focused primarily on the deliverance of the elect and voiced in the name of the entire community. It is these petitions that the rite considers the scrutiny proper, while the exorcism that follows serves to reinforce them (141).

In light of this, the term *scrutiny* makes sense after all. It is a kind of inquiry, but it is a "scrutinizing" that is done by the elect themselves in reflecting on God's word in the presence of the local community, which prays on their behalf. For this reason, scrutinies are called rites of "self-searching and repentance" (141) and culminate in an exorcism— the earnest prayer of the church for the deliverance from evil and for strengthening those soon to be baptized. Their purpose is succinctly described in the introduction to the scrutinies:

The scrutinies are meant to uncover, then heal all that is weak, defective or sinful in the hearts of the elect; to bring out, then strengthen all that is upright, strong and good. For the scrutinies are celebrated in order to deliver the elect from the power of sin and Satan, to protect them against temptation, and to give them strength in Christ, who is the way, the truth and the life (141).

The Readings for the First Scrutiny

Commentaries often emphasize that the readings for the three scrutiny Sundays were chosen by the early church and proposed by the new lectionary because they treat three levels of disorder and sin in human life: the personal (the Samaritan woman), the social (the man born blind) and the cosmic (the raising of Lazarus). The readings for one of these Sundays, then, are meant to provide the opportunity for the baptized community and the elect to focus on one of the three principal ways that sin and evil wound and separate human life from God.

This is one way of relating the three gospel readings and their corresponding scrutinies to each other, but this understanding should not be exaggerated. While there is always a certain focus dictated by the lectionary's choice of readings, it is a mistake to attempt to limit the message to one particular theme such as "personal sin" or "social sin." The readings for the first scrutiny are a case in point.

The reading from Exodus 17:3−7 speaks of the grumbling of the thirsty Israelites in the desert and the miraculous spring of water that issued from the rock at Horeb through the ministry of Moses. This reading is surely an illustration of how the attitudes of society can cause people to doubt God's faithfulness and blind them to the truth about themselves and the world.

The gospel of the Samaritan woman, which usually is taken as an example of individual sin, also must be placed in the context of social sin: The question of worship is abruptly introduced in the narrative after the discussion of living water. Samaritans and Jews, divided by a common history and culture, are unable to agree on something as basic as where to worship God—on Mount Gerizim in Samaria or on

Mount Moriah in Jerusalem. The Gospel of John, while admitting that the Jews do understand what they worship, announces the fulfillment of all legitimate worship of the God in Jesus Christ: "Yet the hour is coming, and is already here, when authentic worshipers will worship the Father in Spirit and in truth." Authentic worship is that in which the worshipers recognize the truth about themselves and about their relationship with God and one another because of Jesus Christ. The prayers for the first scrutiny use the image of an "authentic worshiper" to speak about the consequences of having faced evil and self-delusion with the help of God's grace:

> Lord Jesus,
> in your merciful wisdom
> you touched the heart of the sinful woman
> and taught her to worship the Father
> in spirit and in truth. (154, Exorcism B)

> Show your elect the way of salvation in the Holy Spirit,
> that they may come to worship the Father in truth,
> for you reign for ever and ever. (154, Exorcism A)

The opening prayer, taken from the first of the ritual Masses listed under "Christian Initiation: The Scrutinies" in the sacramentary (cf. RCIA, 146), also makes allusion to the preparation of the elect to enter fully into the worship of the church:

> Lord, you call these chosen ones
> to the glory of a new birth in Christ, the second Adam.
> Help them grow in wisdom and love,
> as they prepare to profess their faith in you.[4]

The social dimensions of sin and salvation are present in the readings of the first scrutiny Mass. Whether the preacher emphasizes these or the more personal aspects of sin should be determined by the most important aspect of the liturgical context, the people celebrating the scrutiny.

The Liturgical Context: The People

Allusion to the specific needs of the elect for deliverance should be made in the celebration of the scrutinies. The most obvious place is in the intercessions. The rite provides for the adaptation of these intentions "to fit the various circumstances" of the elect (RCIA, 153). The intentions as they stand, without adaptation, are very general although they do incorporate some of the issues raised by the readings. To use them without reference to the particular struggles of the elect would be to neglect a powerful opportunity to name the forces that stand in the way of real knowledge of God, self and others.

The sacramentary also offers places for the inclusion of those for and with whom the scrutinies are celebrated. In addition to the presidential prayers from the ritual Masses "Christian Initiation: The Scrutinies," presiders should be aware of the special interpolations for the Roman Canon, one mentioning the godparents and the other that prays for the elect. If other eucharistic prayers are used, it would make a great deal of pastoral sense to include a special intercession for the godparents and sponsors in either the scrutiny intercessions or in the general intercessions, if they are used after the dismissal of the elect and catechumens. The traditional inclusion of prayers for godparents/sponsors during these Sundays underlines the importance that the church places on this ministry.

Ritualization

When preparing for the celebration of the first scrutiny, one must keep in mind that the primary agent in any liturgical rite is the assembly, the people of God. In the introductory paragraphs of the RCIA, they are mentioned specifically as being part of the ministries and offices of the rite: "The faithful should take care to participate in the rites of the scrutinies and presentations and give the elect the example of their own renewal in the spirit of penance, faith and charity" (9.4).

Placement of the Elect and Godparents   Because it is the assembly, led by the presider, that is directing its prayers to God for the elect, any placement of the elect and the godparents that isolates the liturgical action in the sanctuary—as if the priest were the only one "doing" the rite—ritually enacts a misunderstanding of what the scrutiny is about. Many parishes have found it effective to arrange the elect with their godparents in the aisles of the church. In this way, the action of prayer and exorcism is not taking place "up there" in the altar area, but in the midst of God's people.

Posture and Gesture   After explaining the purpose of the scrutiny to the assembly during the homily and then asking for their participation in it, the presider invites them to pray in silence. The rite then calls for the presider to address the elect and to begin the intercessory prayer by inviting them to pray in silence while bowing their heads or kneeling.

Kneeling, a traditional sign of repentance, is certainly appropriate, but because the assembly should be standing at this point (because they are praying *for* the elect), there is the danger that the people for whom they are praying will drop entirely from view. Inviting the elect to stand with their heads bowed is a reasonable alternative.

Silence   The two periods of silence should be ample. If all present understand what they are doing, the concentrated silence of a church full of people at prayer can bear more eloquent testimony to the presence and power of the Spirit than most words. The intercessions for the elect, already discussed, follow.

Exorcism   The intercessory prayer is followed by the exorcism, which is led by the priest or deacon. It is composed of three parts; the first is a prayer addressed to the Father and invokes God's power to heal and protect the elect on their journey. It is followed by a laying on of hands. It is fitting that this rich gesture be done not only by the priest but also by the godparents and other key ministers who have been involved in the conversion process with the elect. The third part of the exorcism is a prayer addressed to Christ, to be offered by the presider with arms outstretched over the elect. Again, to emphasize the communal nature of this act of exorcism, it would be appropriate to invite the entire assembly to extend their hands over the elect with the presider. This gesture is especially effective if the elect are placed in the middle of the assembly.

Conclusion of the Rite

The rite may conclude with an appropriate song. If what has just transpired has touched both assembly and elect, no other conclusion is more fitting, as long as the music reflects the seriousness of what has just taken place. The elect then are to be dismissed as the assembly starts the liturgy of the eucharist.

Candidates for Full Communion

One of the situations faced by catechumenate directors in U.S. parishes is the number of baptized but uncatechized individuals enrolled in the catechumenal process. In these cases, one is not dealing with catechumens or elect, but with candidates seeking the full communion of the Catholic Church. Even a superficial look at the prayers for the scrutinies indicates that they are written for the unbaptized.

The revised rite provides a "Penitential Rite (Scrutiny)" for baptized candidates (459). This rite takes place on the Second Sunday of Lent and follows much the same format as the scrutinies for the elect.

While there is a natural tendency on the part of some candidates to feel neglected or left out if they are not included in the scrutinies, it makes no theological sense to scrutinize baptized persons. To scrutinize candidates can be ecumenically insensitive because it might lead some people to presume that these people's baptisms did not "take."

Instead of ignoring the candidates during the scrutinies, it makes sense to try to include them in the ministry of the assembly. During Lent, the assembly is preparing for the renewal of their own baptismal commitment while praying for their unbaptized sisters and brothers.[5]

Conclusion

A brief review of the early church's understanding of the purpose of the scrutiny celebrations helps to demystify this word, which can easily be misunderstood by the elect and initiation ministers alike. Rather than being a test to determine the sincerity of the elect, these celebrations underline not only the church's dependence on God for all things but also its unshakable confidence that with Jesus Christ human beings can triumph over the evil that seeks to delude and enslave us. It is only through an awareness of our fundamental poverty and dependence on God that we come to the gift of living water that is Jesus Christ—and are able to worship God in spirit and truth.

Notes

[1] From the *Sacramentarium Gelasianum Vetus,* Mohlberg, ed. no. 292; an English translation of this section of the sacramentary is available in E. C. Whitaker, *The Documents of the Baptismal Liturgy* (London: SPCK, 1985), 166–96.

[2] For a fascinating discussion of the role of exorcism in baptismal preparation and liturgical development in the ancient Church, see Henry Anscar Kelly, *The Devil at Baptism: Ritual, Theology, and Drama* (New York: Cornell University Press, 1985).

[3] James Dunning, "Confronting the Demons: The Social Dimension of Conversion," in R. Duggan, ed., *Conversion and the Catechumenate* (New York: Paulist Press, 1984), 30.

[4] The translation of the last line obscures the allusion to worship contained in the original Latin prayer, which more literally defines the goal of preparation as worship: "to come to the public proclamation of your praise" *(ad confessionem tuae laudis accedere).* On the goal of the elect as the worship of God in spirit and in truth, see Adrian Nocent, "L'OICA: Lignes Théologico-liturgiques du catécuménat," *Ephemerides Liturgicae* 88 (1971), 170.

[5] See some of the excellent suggestions offered by Ronald Oakham, "Baptized Candidates and the Lenten Rites," *Catechumenate* (November 1990), 18–25.

7

PRESENTATION
OF THE CREED

A creed is a living statement of faith. From its apostolic origins, the Christian church was a confessing church, possessing a creed in the broadest sense of the term, namely, a commonly held kerygma. Although in the Christian Bible there are no full-blown creeds, there are short creedal fragments such as "Jesus is Lord" (1 Corinthians 12:3, Romans 10:9, Philippians 2:11) that eventually developed into the creeds as we know them.

Dozens of different summaries of faith grew up and mutated in the context of baptism and catechesis. "Mother creeds" like the Roman Baptismal Creed of the second century produced several "daughter creeds," offspring that were scattered across different regions and languages. Many of these creeds arose to correct specific doctrinal errors. This function explains their technical phraseology. While no one creed contains everything there is to say about faith, creeds generally strive to present the essentials. Typically, they are structured according to a trinitarian ground plan, an arrangement that reflects what Christians believe about the God who redeems us through Jesus Christ in the power of the Holy Spirit.

CATHERINE

MOWRY

LACUGNA

The history of the development of creeds is fascinating indeed, like crafting a beautiful mosaic.[1] As we shall see, there are many kinds of creeds and several purposes for creeds. But the focus here is on creeds in connection with baptism, particularly with the catechetical preparation for baptism that today is celebrated in the presentation of the creed in the order of Christian initiation of adults.

The Presentation of the Creed

During the period of purification and enlightenment, after the candidates for baptism have been enrolled as members of the elect, they are "presented" with the faith and prayer of the church in the form of the creed and the Lord's Prayer.

> The creed recalls the wonderful works of God for the salvation of [humankind]. . . . The Lord's Prayer fills [the elect] with a deeper realization of the new spirit of adoption by which they will call God their Father. (RCIA, 147)

The presentations are made after the celebration of the scrutinies, which are ceremonies of exorcism, repentance and conversion. Scrutinies are an opportunity for the elect to make firm their decision to undertake baptism. Scrutinies are also an opportunity for the community to recognize and to pray for the ongoing conversion of the candidates for baptism.

The creed is to be presented during the week following the first scrutiny, that is, the third week of Lent, although many parishes now do so at the Sunday parish liturgy so that the entire community can share in this important aspect of Christian initiation (RCIA, 104–05, 148–49).

In both the baptismal practice of antiquity and the catechumenal process today, there are two points at which the candidate for baptism is to confess his or her faith by means of a creed: as the culmination of the period of catechesis and in the rite of baptism itself. The practice today is consistent with ancient practice on this point.

The Creed in the Rite of Baptism   Prior to the third century, the only
creeds connected with baptism were *interrogatory*. In the *Apostolic Tradition,* written about 215 by Hippolytus, we read:

> When he who is to be baptized goes down to the water, let him
> who baptizes lay hands on him saying this, "Do you believe in
> God the Father almighty?" And he who is being baptized shall
> say, "I believe." Let him baptize him once, having his hand laid
> upon his head.

> After this let him say, "Do you believe in Christ Jesus, the Son of
> God, Who was born by the Holy Spirit from the Virgin Mary,
> who was crucified under Pontius Pilate and died, and rose again
> on the third day living from the dead, and ascended into the
> heavens, and sat down at the right hand of the Father and will
> come to judge the living and the dead?" And when he says, "I
> believe," let him baptize him the second time.

> And again let him say, "Do you believe in the Holy Spirit, in the
> holy church and the resurrection of the flesh?" And he who is
> being baptized shall say, "I believe." And so let him baptize him
> the third time.

The triple interrogation, the triple affirmation and the triple immersion
in water reflected the trinitarian pattern of Christian faith, specifically,
the threefold name into which Christians are baptized (cf. Matthew
28:19).

The Creed and Catechesis   The second type of creed is *declaratory*.
A declaratory creed is a statement of faith in the first person ("I/we
believe . . .") using a fixed pattern of words. Declaratory creeds originated probably in the third century as a by-product of the catechetical
stage of Christian initiation. It would have been natural to recapitulate
the essentials of Christian faith in a short formula for the benefit of those
preparing for baptism. Though the declaratory creeds played a central
role in catechetical instruction, they were not connected with the water
rite. This is why the *Rite of Christian Initiation of Adults* prescribes the
declaratory form of the creed for the presentations.

   In the ancient church, the bishop solemnly "handed over" *(traditio)*
the creed by asking the elect to listen as the faithful recited it. Later the

elect "handed back" *(redditio)* the creed by reciting it publicly before the bishop and the faithful. The creed was understood as a secret formula, not to be written down. The recitation of the creed publicly by the elect was a sign that the bishop considered their faith was strong enough for baptism. Today, the RCIA contains similar rites of *traditio* (183–87) and *redditio* (194–99). Baptismal candidates are expected to learn the creed (and the Lord's Prayer) by heart and recite it (them) publicly as a sign of reddition.

Which Creed to Use?

The baptismal creed was called a *symbol* of faith (*symbolum* = token or reminder). At first, the term *symbol* denoted the baptismal questions and answers; later on, "symbol" became the regular title of the declaratory creed.[2]

The Apostles' Creed, the Nicene Creed and the Creed of Constantinople[3] are declaratory creeds, symbols of the God into whose name we are baptized. Any one of these creeds may be "presented" to today's catechumens. To make them clearer to compare, the following four creeds are presented in literal translations from ancient Greek and Latin critical editions, rather than in more familiar adaptations.

Roman Baptismal Creed
(second century)

I believe in God the Father almighty;

and in Christ Jesus his only Son,
    our Lord,
Who was born from the Holy Spirit
    and the Virgin Mary,
Who under Pontius Pilate was
    crucified and buried,
on the third day rose again from
    the dead,

Apostles' Creed
(sixth or seventh century)

I believe in God the Father almighty,
    creator of heaven and earth;
And in Jesus Christ, his only Son, our
    Lord, who was conceived by the
    Holy Spirit, born from the Virgin
    Mary, suffered under Pontius
    Pilate, was crucified, dead and
    buried, descended to hell, on the
    third day rose again from the
    dead, ascended to heaven, sits at
    the right hand of God the Father

ascended to heaven,
sits at the right hand of the Father,
    whence he will
    come to judge the living and
    the dead;
and in the Holy Spirit,
the holy church,
the remission of sins,
    the resurrection of the flesh.

almighty, thence he will come to
judge the living and the dead;

I believe in the Holy Spirit, the holy
    catholic church, the communion
    of saints, the remission of sins, the
    resurrection of the flesh, and
    eternal life.

Nicene Creed (325)

Creed of Constantinople (381)

(Sometimes called Nicene Creed, Nicene-
Constantinopolitan Creed or Ecumenical
Creed)

We believe in one God, the Father,
    almighty,
    maker of all things visible and
    invisible;

And in one Lord Jesus Christ, the Son
    of God, begotten from the
    Father, only-begotten, that is,
    from the substance of the Father,
    God from God, light from true
    light, true God from true God,
    begotten not made, of one sub-
    stance with the Father, through
    Whom all things came into
    being, things in heaven and
    things on earth, Who because of
    us and because of our salvation
    came down and became incar-
    nate, becoming human *(enanthro-
    pesanta)*, suffered and rose again
    on the third day, ascended to the
    heavens, will come to judge the
    living and the dead;

We believe in one God, the Father,
    almighty,
    maker of heaven and earth, of all
    things
    visible and invisible;

And in one Lord Jesus Christ, the
    only-begotten Son of God,
    begotten from the Father before
    all ages, light from light, true
    God from true God, begotten
    not made, of one substance with
    the Father, through Whom all
    things came into existence, Who
    because of us and because of our
    salvation came down from
    heaven, and was incarnate from
    the Holy Spirit and the Virgin
    Mary and became human *(enan-
    thropesanta)*, and was crucified for
    us under Pontius Pilate, and
    suffered and was buried, and rose
    again on the third day according
    to the Scriptures and ascended to
    heaven, and sits on the right hand
    of the Father, and will come

And in the Holy Spirit;
But as for those who say, there was a
time when (the Son) was not,
and, before being born (the Son)
was not, and that (the Son) came
into existence out of nothing, or
who assert that the Son of God is
of a different hypostasis or substance, or is subject to alteration
or change—these the catholic
and apostolic church
anathematizes.

again with glory to judge the
living and dead, of Whose
kingdom there will be no end.
And in the Holy Spirit, the Lord and
life-giver, who proceeds from the
Father, who with the Father and
the Son is together worshiped and
together glorified, who spoke
through the prophets; in one holy
catholic and apostolic church. We
confess one baptism to the remission of sins; we look forward to
the resurrection of the dead and
the life of the world to come.

The Apostles' Creed is, in fact, a descendant of the Roman Baptismal Creed, which originated in the second century.[4] The usual version of the Apostles' Creed, which came to function in the West as the sole baptismal creed, probably originated in the late sixth or seventh century.[5] Martin Luther, John Calvin and Ulrich Zwingli affirmed the Apostles' Creed as a binding summary of faith and doctrine. In the Anglican church, it was recited twice a day, at morning and evening prayer.

A glance at the texts of the Apostles' Creed and the Ecumenical Creed shows that while both are structured by the same trinitarian ground plan, there are major differences between them. The Apostles' Creed is a narrative of the events of salvation history; there is no speculation about the preexistence of Christ, nor is the divinity of the Holy Spirit explicitly affirmed. In contrast, several phrases in the Ecumenical Creed, with which we are so familiar, are aimed at specific heresies that arose in the fourth century. This creed of 381 affirms that Christ is "of the same substance" as God and that the Holy Spirit is to be worshiped as God.

From just this one example it is evident that creeds are living documents that develop as the situation (such as a new heresy) demands. The Ecumenical Creed is more explicitly theological and doctrinal, using language that carefully rules out certain interpretations of faith. The easy narrative style of the Apostles' Creed and its freedom from particular doctrinal debates gives it an immediacy that the Ecumenical Creed does not have. The Apostles' Creed is therefore an attractive choice for the presentations.

But the Apostles' Creed is virtually unknown in the Eastern church and never was used for its baptism, even though it was routinely used in the Western church. Eastern churches use the Ecumenical Creed exclusively. This is an important consideration for those who value ecumenical consensus.[6] The Ecumenical Creed is one of the few things that East and West hold in common.[7] If it is used for the presentations, the candidate will be explicitly united with the wider community: the Orthodox, Roman Catholic, Anglican and other churches.

Teaching the Creed

Many declaratory creeds have been formulated throughout history, some of which are widely accepted as normative, others of which are strictly regional (e.g., fourth-century Spanish baptismal creeds) or denominational (e.g., the Augsburg Confession of 1530). Regardless of which creed is presented to the candidate for baptism, the following should be kept in mind.

The purpose of presenting the creed (and Lord's Prayer) is to *teach*. Tradition *(traditio)* is less a repository of teachings than a *means* of instruction. Therefore, the catechist, minister or homilist should use the presentations to teach the entire congregation, not just the baptismal candidates, the meaning of the creed.

The creed has meaning in at least two respects: its content and its form. With respect to content, there are several good commentaries on creeds.[8] Studying the origins and individual elements of creeds gives Christians and Christians-to-be an informed picture of the origins of their faith. Studying more than just the statements of faith can create a strong sense of connection to the universal church throughout the world and throughout time, just as baptism unites us with believers before us and after us and with those today who live across national and linguistic boundaries.

On form, creeds are living statements of faith. Reciting a creed is more than memorization and repetition of a dusty document; even less is it mindless assent to unintelligible propositions. Confessing a creed is supposed to be doxological, that is, an act of praise and thanksgiving for what God has done in salvation history. It is easier with the Apostles' Creed than with the Creed of Constantinople to appreciate the doxological nature of creeds.

It cannot be emphasized strongly enough that Christians do not believe in the generic God of theism or deism but in the God of Jesus Christ. Creeds are the confession of concrete faith, mediated by specific symbols that bind a believer to a particular story of salvation. Likewise, Christians are not baptized into "God in general" but into the mystery of God disclosed in the economy of a particular redemptive history, under the name, Father, Son, Spirit.

There are sound theological, historical, liturgical and pastoral reasons for retaining either the Apostles' Creed or the Ecumenical Creed in the presentations. No other creed should be used for the *traditio* or *redditio*.

But for other occasions, there is every reason to encourage the articulation of contemporary restatements of apostolic faith. Often the language, ideas and context of ancient creeds are hard to grasp today. The fear that contemporary historical and scientific knowledge could render the creed difficult for modern people to believe prompted Pope Paul VI in 1967 to promulgate the "Credo of the People of God," a reformulation of the essentials of the faith of the apostles.[9] Hundreds of other modern creeds and confessional statements have appeared, such as the short statements of theologians like Karl Rahner,[10] creedal statements of certain groups or coalitions (e.g., feminist or pacifist) that highlight a particular dimension of faith, statements endorsed by particular church groups (such as a local bishops' conference) or statements of ecumenical church groups seeking wide agreement on basic doctrinal points.[11] These new creeds help us to see the dynamic and adaptive nature of creeds as declarations of faith. For example, there are creeds from Catholic base communities in El Salvador, from the Presbyterian church in South Africa and from the Baptist Union in Switzerland.[12]

Those who are preparing for baptism should be encouraged to study different kinds of creeds and then formulate their own declaration of faith. Though personal creeds are not a substitute for the enduring creeds of antiquity, still, it is important that the elect preparing for baptism participate actively in the confession of their faith. *Credo* is the opening line of the lifelong conversation between ourselves and God, as well as a public proclamation of how we see ourselves in relation to the human community, for which baptism is the outward sacramental sign.

Notes

[1] The best source for the history of creeds is J. N. D. Kelly's *Early Christian Creeds,* 3d ed. (London: Longman, 1972), and his *The Athanasian Creed* (New York: Harper & Row, 1964). There also are several collections of various creeds and confessional statements that may be consulted.

[2] Kelly, *Early Christian Creeds,* 60.

[3] As the texts of the creeds show, the Nicene Creed and the Constantinople Creed are distinct; the latter was promulgated 56 years after the Council of Nicaea. The third article of the Nicene Creed reads simply, "And in the Holy Spirit." The divinity of the Spirit was not officially taught until 381 at the Council of Constantinople. The Constantinople Creed of 381 (the creed frequently used at Mass), ironically, often is referred to as the Nicene Creed; to avoid confusion, some also call the Constantinople Creed the Ecumenical Creed.

[4] Kelly, *Early Christian Creeds,* 3.

[5] *Ibid.,* 420.

[6] The ancient creeds contain all that is necessary for Christian faith. It is noteworthy that none of these creeds contains any reference to those dogmas solemnly defined

within Roman Catholicism many centuries later, such as papal infallibility or the Assumption and Immaculate Conception of Mary, and no reference to other doctrinal disputes such as transubstantiation or justification by faith alone.

[7] This is true despite the fact that the West unilaterally inserted into the Constantinople Creed the *filioque* clause ("the Spirit proceeds from the Father *and* from the Son"). Many theologians today recommend that Western churches drop this clause, thereby preventing further offense to the Orthodox.

[8] Some recent commentaries include Bernard Marthaler, *The Creed* (Mystic: Twenty-Third Publications, 1987); N. Ayo, *The Creed As Symbol* (Notre Dame: University of Notre Dame Press, 1989); H.-G. Link, *One God, One Lord, One Spirit,* Faith and Order Paper No. 139 (Geneva: World Council of Churches Publications, 1988).

[9] The text is in *The Pope Speaks* 13 (1968), 273–82.

[10] Karl Rahner, *Foundations of Christian Faith* (New York: Crossroad, 1983), 448–60.

[11] These are summarized by Avery Dulles, "Foundation Documents of the Faith," *Expository Times* 91 (1980), 291–99. *Expository Times* carries 11 brief essays on various creeds, in vol. 91/1–3 (1979), vol. 91/4–11 (1980); contributors are P. R. Ackroyd, J. G. Davies, J. Macquarrie, G. Rupp, D. Fenlon, C. W. Dygmore, J. K. S. Reid, W. M. S. West, A. R. George, A. Dulles, W. Pannenberg.

[12] *Confessing Our Faith Around the World,* 4 vols., ed. H.-G. Link (Geneva: World Council of Churches Publications, 1983–).

8

I ONCE WAS BLIND AND NOW I SEE: SECOND SCRUTINY

He healed the darkness of my mind
The day he gave my sight to me:
It was not sin that made me blind:
It was no sinner made me see.

Let others call my faith a lie,
Or try to stir up doubt in me:
Look at me now! None can deny
I once was blind and now I see!

Ask me not how! But I know who
Has opened up new worlds to me:
This Jesus does what none can do—
I once was blind, and now I see.[1]

The hymn "He healed the darkness of my mind" by Fred Pratt Green, based on the gospel of the man born blind, poetically summarizes the faith dynamics of the second scrutiny: the forces of darkness raging against the life of faith; the elect encountering the illuminating power of Christ; and the church community clarifying, accepting and confirming its encounter with the demonic and the divine.

Many commentators have pointed to the confrontation with "social sin" at the heart of the second scrutiny. While no liturgical event can be reduced to a single message, these readings and rites do force us to acknowledge the "mystery of iniquity" in the light of God's liberating power in Christ:

- that we are born into a broken world whose shattered character we confirm and extend with our own selfish choices;

MICHAEL JONCAS

- that we are born into a broken world whose shattered character we confirm and extend with our own selfish choices;
- that we are shaped to a great degree by sociobiological factors that condition, color and seemingly control our response to reality;
- that unmasking our self-destructive and other destructive behaviors and their deep complicity with evil is laborious and stoutly resisted both culturally and personally;
- that naming these behaviors as "sins," symptomatic of our profound alienation from creation, others, ourselves and God, is actually a gift—discernment—given by the Spirit;
- and that the disclosure of our sin need not crush us but rather can call us to conversion and transformation by the power of Christ.

The following pastoral-liturgical commentary on the second scrutiny presupposes that these dynamics will be ritually celebrated on the Fourth Sunday of Lent using the readings of Year A. I will comment on the scriptures appointed for proclamation, which set the context for the ritual action, the verbal dimensions of the rite, the musical dimensions of the rite and the kinetic dimensions of the rite.

The Scriptures of the Fourth Sunday of Lent, Year A

The gospel of the man born blind (John 9:1–41) dominates the liturgy of the word on the Fourth Sunday of Lent. The social implications of complicity with evil are embodied in the Pharisees and the blind man's parents: religious leaders choosing ideological safety over the evidence of God's benevolence, kin ostracizing their flesh and blood for fear of social reprisal. The Johannine irony is especially pointed: Those who should be most clear-sighted cannot correctly interpret the plain evidence, while the man born blind (nameless, as befits an "Everyman" character) cuts through all the specious arguments by clinging to his experience of Jesus. The gospel is both a fierce warning to the faithful lest they betray Jesus' message with "pious" language and behavior that avoid his call to life-giving service and a realistic caution to the elect about the social implications of their faith in the Lord. Seeing the world through Jesus' eyes will overturn accustomed ways of evaluating reality.

Ephesians 5:8–14 also strongly emphasizes the moral implications of being illuminated by Christ. Notice the plural: "Live as *children* of light." Personal conversion to Jesus' vision implies being part of a community of disciples whose corporate witness challenges the powers of darkness.

Psalm 23 mediates between the conversion themes of the John and Ephesians readings and the election themes of the 1 Samuel reading. While the Hebrew tradition identified the Lord (YHWH) as the shepherd and host who nourishes and protects, Christians addressed the same text to Jesus as their "Good Shepherd" and eucharistic Lord. They saw in the psalm's images of water, table and oil clear references to baptism, eucharist and chrismation. Perhaps the strongest resonance generated by this psalm in the second scrutiny appears in verse four, where descent into the "valley of the shadow of death" is recognized as the lot of all human beings, a lot made bearable by a God who chooses to walk with us in the darkness, guiding our footsteps and staving off the enemy.

The story of the election and anointing of David (1 Samuel 16:1, 6–7, 10–13) points out the contrast between human and divine judgment: "People do not see as God sees, because people see the appearance but the Lord looks into the heart." Just as David, the least important, is chosen by God's free initiative, so the elect have been chosen by God's grace. But precisely because God sees into our divided hearts, it is appropriate that the church bring the elect to the rituals of illumination and purification called "scrutinies."

Frankly, the richness of these scriptures proclaimed may be too intense for some local communities. Rather than shortening the Gospel, it might be appropriate to omit either the 1 Samuel or the Ephesians reading. Another possibility might be to reposition the Ephesians reading as a charge to the catechumens when they are dismissed after the exorcism prayer and/or song,[2] or as the final dismissal addressed to the entire assembly.

Verbal Dimensions of the Rite

Intercessions   Two formularies are provided as models for adaptation of the intercessions for the elect. Set A provides four intercessions for the elect, two for those persecuted for or prevented from embracing Christian faith, one for the church in its countercultural stance and one for the spiritual liberty of the world. Set B provides six intercessions for the elect (strongly emphasizing "light" themes from the scriptures proclaimed), one for the church and one for the world's inhabitants. The first set seems more abstract, the second more poetic; thus, the second set may provide more appropriate texts for chanting.

Notice that if the elect are dismissed, the general intercessions and/or profession of faith may follow. While it is historically and theologically correct to dismiss the elect before the baptized engage in their priestly prayer for the needs of the world, pastoral practice indicates that some communities find a "second" prayer of the faithful, whose focus is universal needs rather than intercession for the elect, to be redundant. If the intercessions for the elect are fused with the "prayer of the faithful," planners must be sensitive to both the length and the style of the intercessions; the proportions of both model sets (four each for the elect and general needs in the first set, six for the elect and two for general needs in the second) indicate a ritual preference and pattern.

Exorcism   Two formularies for an exorcism immediately follow the intercessions. The exorcisms exhibit a threefold structure: a presidential prayer addressed to the Father that the elect be freed from the powers of darkness, concluded by the assembly's "Amen"; a laying of hands by the celebrant on each of the elect (presumably in silence); and a presidential prayer addressed to Jesus asking that the Holy Spirit be poured out on the elect, concluded by the assembly's "Amen." Formulary A is more succinct and abstract, Formulary B more image-laden and evocative, but they are not strictly correlated with the two preceding intercessory formularies: Either Formulary A or B could be used after either set of intercessions.

It could be argued that the prayer addressed to the Father really functions as the conclusion of the intercessions while also serving as a bridge to the laying on of hands, whose meaning, in turn, is specified by the Christ-centered and Spirit-invoking concluding prayer. If so, the presider might want to indicate the different qualities of these prayers not only by his gestures (hands joined or in *orans* position [See the section "Kinetic Dimensions of the Rite" later in this article.] versus hands outstretched over the elect) but also by chanting one and speaking the other.

Mass Euchology   In addition to the texts intimately associated with the scrutiny rite itself, the minor Mass euchology (opening prayer, prayer over the gifts, prayer after communion, solemn blessing/prayer over the people) and major Mass euchology (preface, eucharistic prayer) make their own contributions to this liturgical celebration.

One might choose the minor euchology either from the Mass for the Fourth Sunday of Lent or from the ritual Mass for the second scrutiny; as one would expect, the prayers of the Sunday formulary are more universal in tone, while those of the ritual Mass focus on the elect. The prayer after communion of the Sunday formulary is especially felicitous in pointing up the "illumination" imagery stemming from the Gospel proclamation.

The preface of the Fourth Sunday of Lent (P15) beautifully inter-weaves the themes of enlightenment and initiation; the acknowledgment of Christ's power to liberate us not only from our sins but from Sin itself leads us to praise our loving God. Praying this preface suggests using either Eucharistic Prayer I or III for the rest of the anaphora;[3] the ritual Mass for the scrutinies provides special insertions for Eucharistic Prayer I commemorating the elect and (by name) the godparents of the elect.

Musical Dimensions of the Rite

Responsorial Psalm: Psalm 23   While the *General Instruction of the Roman Missal,* 36, declares that the gradual is "an integral part of the liturgy of the word," the English term "responsorial psalm" has proven confusing for liturgical commentators and pastoral planners. This element is not a response to the first reading nor is it a meditation song. The responsorial psalm is a scriptural proclamation in its own right, a *sung* scriptural proclamation just as the "Prophet," "Apostle" and "Gospel" are (normally) *read* scriptural proclamations. Just as the other scriptural readings are proclaimed by their proper ministers (lector, deacon or priest), with congregational acclamations ("Thanks be to God"; "Glory to you, O Lord"; "Praise to you, Lord Jesus Christ"), so the gradual is proclaimed by its own proper minister, the cantor, with congregational interventions (the "antiphon" refrain). The term "responsorial" refers to the format the psalm takes in the lectionary (that is, provided with a "response") rather than a description of its function in the liturgy of the word.

Although the official liturgical books express a preference for sung congregational participation in the gradual, there are six formats in which it might be executed: first, "solo direct," in which the psalm is sung entirely by a cantor without any intervention by the assembly; second, "choir direct," in which the psalm is sung entirely by a choir/schola without any intervention by the assembly (this is the format in which the Latin *gradual* is normally sung); third, "assembly direct," in which the psalm is sung entirely by the assembly without refrains or alternation; fourth, "responsorial," in which the assembly interjects a refrain after strophes of the psalm are sung by a cantor and/or choir (this seems to be the most common format in the United States); fifth, "alternating," in which the psalm is sung in alternating strophes between two sections of the assembly (a typical monastic method of chanting psalms at the Divine Office); and sixth, "experimental/mixed," in which various combinations of the other formats, speaking or instrumental interludes might appear. As long as the primacy of the proclamation of the text is maintained, the choice of format is contingent on the resources available to the local community.

Gospel Acclamation The gospel greeting (John 8:12) acclaims the word of God as "light of the world." Given the length of the gospel reading, the musical setting of the acclamation should be to scale. For example, a procession with the Book of the Gospels (evangeliary) preceded by a procession with candles as the gospel acclamation is being sung could point up the illumination themes of the gospel text.

Intercessions Because the intercessions for the elect take the form of variable intentions pronounced by an assisting minister, each followed with an invariable refrain by the assembly, litanic and mantra musical settings of these texts may enhance their power. The simplest format would consist of a deacon/cantor singing the intercession on a single pitch *(recto tono)* or according to a recitation formula composed for the grammatical and accentual pattern of the text, with a musical "cue formula" on the words "Let us pray to the Lord." In both cases, the assembly would respond with a simple refrain ("Lord, hear our prayer"; "Lord, have mercy"; "Lord in your mercy, hear our prayer"), perhaps overlapping the "Lord" of the cue formula with the initial "Lord" of their response, after the model of the Byzantine *ektene.* A second musical format would be to establish an intercessory mantra ("O Lord, hear my prayer" from the music of Taizé, for example); the assembly (or just the choir) could hum the mantra melody under the spoken or sung intercession and then the assembly could sing the mantra text as a response. In either format, music can clarify the "call/response" pattern of the intercessions for the elect and add solemnity to this time of communal prayer.

Exorcism As already mentioned, one way to distinguish the character of the presidential prayer addressed to the Father from that addressed to Christ would be by chanting one of the prayers and reciting the other.

Traditionally, the Roman Rite has emphasized the laying on of hands by directing that it be done *in silence* (cf. rites of anointing of the sick and ordination). Musicians should resist the impulse to cover this silence with instrumental or vocal "fillers."

Song to Conclude the Scrutiny The rite suggests Psalms 6, 26, 32, 38, 39, 40, 51, 116:1−9, 130, 139 and 142. Inviting the assembly to sing a hymn correlated to the scrutiny rite and the scriptures proclaimed (perhaps with one verse sung by the elect alone) could serve as a musical "profession of faith" before the elect are dismissed. In addition to "He healed the darkness of my mind" printed at the beginning of this article, "Amazing grace" (*Worship III*, 583), "I heard the voice of Jesus say" (*Worship III*, 607), "Awake, O sleeper, rise from death" (*Worship III*, 586), "Awake, O sleeper" (*Gather*, 330), "I want to walk as a child of the light" (*Gather*, 208) or "We are walking in the light" (*Gather*, 207) might be considered.

Kinetic Dimensions of the Rite

There are four sets of people whose "choreography" must be coordinated for the scrutiny to communicate most powerfully: the elect, their godparents, the presiding minister and the assembly. Foremost are the elect with their godparents. The rite directs that they are to come forward out of the assembly and stand before the presiding minister at the conclusion of the homily. This gathering appears to be somewhat informal in that the elect and their godparents are not called by name. While they are in motion, the presider could informally direct the assembly to silent prayer for the elect as the rite indicates. Once the elect and their godparents have assembled, the presider calls the elect to silent prayer as well.

The rite suggests that the elect bow their heads or kneel at this point; kneeling seems to be the stronger posture. (There may be communities where inviting the elect to prostrate during the silent prayer may be appropriate, although it may appear too "theatrical" for most American congregations.) Positioning the godparent slightly behind each of the kneeling elect will facilitate the placing of the godparent's hand on the elect's shoulder during the intercessions. The rite does not call for the assembly to assume the same posture as the elect. Although one could argue that having the members of the assembly bow their heads or kneel in prayer would show solidarity with the elect, giving the elect a different posture than the rest of the assembly better conveys that the elect are the ritual focus of this prayer. Once the various postures are assumed, the presider should allow an extended silence to settle on the group.

After the silent prayer, all stand. The godparents place their right hands on the shoulders of the elect; this is a vivid sign of the godparents' roles as personal support to the candidates and as the community's delegates. In some communities, the presider may turn to face in the same direction as the rest of the assembly during the intercessions to show his solidarity in their common prayer; only at the end of the intercessions would he turn back to face the elect and pray the first exorcism prayer, which is addressed to God the Father. Although the rite directs that this presidential prayer be said with hands joined, commentators have strongly suggested that the presiding minister pray in the *orans* position as he does for other liturgical prayers addressed to the Father.

The rite then directs the presider to lay hands on the elect "if convenient." The presider placing both hands on each elect's head for an extended silent prayer should be considered the norm. Although the rite does not so state, having godparents and other people significant in the candidate's faith journey join in the laying on of hands may be an appropriate pastoral adaptation. Obscuring the godparents' role or turning the rite into a popularity contest based on the number of people coming forward to lay on hands are possible drawbacks to this adaptation.

The rite directs that the presiding minister pray the exorcism prayer addressed to Christ "with hands outstretched over all the elect"; although the rite does not suggest it, inviting the assembly to join in this gesture may symbolize their share in the presidential prayer made in their name.

Notes

[1] Fred Pratt Green, "He healed the darkness of my mind," (Carol Stream IL: Hope Publishing Company, 1982). This text appears yoked to the hymn-tune DUNEDIN

by Thomas V. Griffiths in *Worship: A Hymnal and Service Book for Roman Catholics,* ed. by Robert J. Batastini, third ed. (Chicago IL: GIA Publications, 1986), #749. Because the text is in long meter (8.8. 8.8.), other more familiar hymn-tunes in this meter (e.g., CONDITOR ALME SIDERUM, ERHALT UNS HERR, JESU DULCIS MEMORIA, O WALY WALY, OLD ONE HUNDREDTH, TALLIS' CANON) might be substituted.

[2] For example, "There was a time when you were darkness, but a time is coming when you will be light in the Lord. Well, then, live as children of the light . . . "

[3] As the Consilium's 1968 document *Au cours des derniers mois* notes: "The Roman Canon [Eucharistic Prayer I], which may always be used, must take precedence on feast days that have proper texts as part of the anaphora . . . Eucharistic Prayer III may be joined with any preface already existing in the Roman Missal. On Sundays, therefore, this prayer and the Roman Canon could be alternated."

Because Eucharistic Prayer II "can be used to advantage on weekdays and in Masses with children, young people, and small groups" and Eucharistic Prayer IV "must be used just as it is, without any change even of the preface," these anaphoras would be less appropriate. (International Commission on English in the Liturgy, *Documents on the Liturgy 1963–1979: Conciliar, Papal, and Curial Texts* [Collegeville MN: The Liturgical Press, 1982], #1959, 1961, 1960, 1962, pp. 618–9.)

Similar reasoning suggests that the Eucharistic Prayers for Masses with Children or for Masses of Reconciliation would be inappropriate because they do not accommodate the proper preface of the Fourth Sunday of Lent.

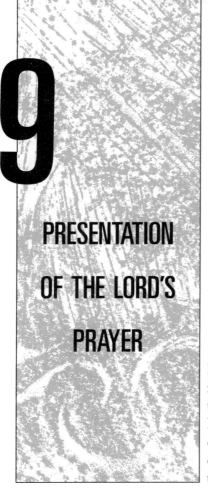

9

PRESENTATION
OF THE LORD'S
PRAYER

No words have inspired more commentaries, sermons, theological treatises, music and poetry than the Lord's Prayer. The oldest commentaries were catechetical instructions for baptismal candidates, because the Lord's Prayer together with the Creed belonged—

and still belong—to the *arcanum,* the "arcane discipline" to which only those already in the church and those in the process of joining the church were privy.

Tertullian, a third-century Latin theologian, considered the Lord's Prayer the "brief summary of the whole gospel" *(breviarium totius evangelii),* containing the essentials of the teaching of Jesus and the model of prayer for all Christians.[1] A long tradition of theological and spiritual writings used the elements of the Lord's Prayer to schematize and recapitulate the main elements of the Christian life. The Greek Fathers in particular linked the Lord's Prayer with the view of Christian life as an ascent into the presence of God through union with Christ and transformation by the Spirit into the perfect image of God. Thomas Aquinas (thirteenth century) wrote in his commentary: "The Lord's Prayer contains all that is to be desired and all that we ought to avoid."[2] The Lord's Prayer is indeed a

CATHERINE

MOWRY

LACUGNA

"perfect" prayer inasmuch as it balances praising and glorifying God with making petitions on our own behalf.

The Lord's Prayer in the New Testament and Early Worship

Luke 11:2–4

Father,
hallowed be thy name.
Thy kingdom come.

Give us each day our daily bread;
and forgive us our sins,
for we ourselves forgive every one
   who is indebted to us;
and lead us not into temptation. (RSV)

Matthew 6:9–13

Our Father who art in heaven,
Hallowed be thy name.
Thy kingdom come,
Thy will be done,
   On earth as it is in heaven.
Give us this day our daily bread;
And forgive us our debts
  As we also have forgiven
   our debtors;
And lead us not into temptation,
But deliver us from evil. (RSV)

There is no consensus among exegetes about whether Matthew's or Luke's version more closely represents the teaching or prayer of Jesus. On the one hand, Luke's version is favored because it is shorter: It contains only five compared with Matthew's seven petitions. Likely the two versions were shaped by different liturgical traditions in distinct geographical and social circumstances. This may explain Matthew's addition of two petitions as well as the addition of the concluding doxology in the *Didache* and in other early liturgical texts.

On the other hand, the wording of Luke's petitions shows the influence of gentile churches (Luke uses "sins" rather than "debts") and a theology adapted to a young church no longer expecting an imminent end (Luke's version asks for bread "day by day" whereas the grammatical structure of Matthew indicates a plea for a once-for-all giving of bread "this day"). While many biblical scholars see the Lucan number of petitions and the Matthean wording as older,[3] the liturgical tradition of the church, especially in connection with baptism, has generally given Matthew's version primacy of place.

The Lord's Prayer was recited frequently by early Christians; the *Didache* (written about 100) instructed believers to recite the Lord's Prayer three times daily. Though most Catholic Christians today associate the Lord's Prayer with the eucharist, its use there did not occur before the mid-fourth century. It always was used, however, in the baptismal setting, as documents such as the *Didache* and others indicate.

Matthew's and Luke's texts show that the doxology was not originally part of the Lord's Prayer, nor is it found in the most reliable New Testament manuscripts. It was common in Judaism, however, to conclude prayers with a formal doxology, and Christian prayer is in large part derived from Judaism. The *Didache* concludes the Lord's Prayer with the doxology, "For to you belongs power and glory into eternity" (*Didache* 8,2); this is probably based on 1 Chronicles 29:11:

> To you, O Lord, belongs the greatness and the power and the glory and the victory and the majesty; for all that is in the heavens and on the earth belongs to you; yours is the rule, O Lord, and you are exalted as head above all.

The liturgical history of the Lord's Prayer shows the church to be greatly flexible, adapting the Lord's Prayer to various liturgical settings. Whether or not the doxology is to be recited outside the eucharist depends on the context and on the traditions of those praying. If it serves the purpose of the praise of God, certainly it should be included. That no doxology was included in the earliest manuscripts of the gospels may evidence simply the difference between a context of instruction and a context of worship.

Presenting the Lord's Prayer to the Elect

As a way of "passing on" *(paradosis, traditio)* the faith and prayer of the church to the elect, the Creed and the Lord's Prayer normally are "presented" to those preparing for baptism so that they may become full and active members of the Christian community. Accordingly, "The Lord's Prayer fills [the elect] with a deeper realization of the new spirit of adoption by which they will call God their Father, especially in the midst of the eucharistic assembly" (RCIA, 147).

The presentations ordinarily take place during the period of purification and enlightenment, when the catechumen has become a member of the elect. The rite directs that the presentations be made after the celebration of the first and third scrutinies, usually celebrated on the Third and Fifth Sundays of Lent (RCIA, 148–49). But for pastoral reasons, the presentations may be held at any point during the catechumenate when the catechumens are judged ready for these celebrations (RCIA, 104–5).

Although all catechumens should have memorized both the Lord's Prayer and the Creed, the emphasis both for the elect *and* for the community at large should be placed less on "recital" and more on "thoughtful praying." When the elect are presented with the Lord's Prayer, the catechist-minister might consider asking each one to write her or his own "gloss" on each petition, such as the following by Karl Rahner.[4] In this way, praying the Lord's Prayer becomes a creedal statement, a declaration of one's belief and a testimony to how one understands what it means to *live* the prayer:

> *Our Father* who are in the depths of my heart, transforming its emptiness into a heaven on earth
> *Hallowed be thy name,* even in the death-like silence of my ignorance and my lack of faith
> *Thy kingdom come* in the midst of my desolation
> *Thy will be done* in me, for thy will is my true life
> *Give us this day our daily bread,* for I am utterly dependent upon thy divine providence
> *Forgive us our trespasses*—those sins that are ultimately treason against thy love for us, and therefore treason against myself
> *Deliver us from evil*—from the evil of centering our lives upon ourselves, in order that we may learn that thou art the center of all and that only in thee can we find freedom worthy of the sons and daughters of God.

The presentations are a splendid opportunity for the homilist to focus on the Lord's Prayer (and the Creed). Effective use could be made of any of the hundreds of commentaries on the Lord's Prayer, especially those by the most perceptive and prayerful theologians, teachers and mystics, such as Tertullian, Origen, Gregory of Nyssa, Augustine, Maximus the Confessor, Bonaventure, Thomas Aquinas, Luther, Catherine of Siena and Teresa of Avila. Most of these are available in good English translations, and they contain startling contemporary insights into both the blessings and the obstacles entailed in the constant conversion required for Christian life.

Praying the Petitions

The Lord's Prayer is a faith-filled plea for God's action in us and in human history. The tenor of the prayer is strongly eschatological (concerned with the end of time). It is difficult for many today, separated by two millennia from the times and mind-set of the early followers of Jesus, to appreciate just how ardently they longed for Christ's immediate return in glory. According to the synoptic gospels, both God's "Fatherhood" and our status as sons and daughters of God would not be realized until the reign of God had been fully realized.[5] At first, Christians expected this end to occur in their own lifetimes (Mark 9:1), and Matthew may intend this. Gradually, the sense of urgency gave way to the sense that the reign of God is both future and already realized, both in the person of Jesus and in the new community of Christ's followers.

Our Father Who Art in Heaven   In the Bible and in early creeds, "Father" was a synonym for God.[6] By addressing God as Father, we acknowledge both the transcendence of God who "dwells in light inaccessible," and the immanence (nearness) of the Creator who initiates the covenant with Israel and whom we encounter in Christ. Bold as it may be to proclaim God as our Father, it is the Spirit praying in us who enables us to address God as intimately as Jesus did when he called God "Abba" (Romans 8:15; Galatians 4:6).

We call upon God as *our* Father, not *my* Father. Augustine remarked that the emperor as well as the beggar, the slave as well as the master can say in common "Our Father." By this they show themselves to be brothers and sisters to each other in Christ.[7] It would violate the name of God as "Father" if we were to use that name to exclude others, to justify sin or to maintain a divided community. The Father whom we address in the Lord's Prayer is the living God whom Jesus proclaimed, not the God of our fantasies, whether patriarchal or otherwise.[8] In Christ, through baptism, all previous divisions (male-female, slave-free, Jew-gentile) give way to new unity in the Spirit. One sign of Christian conversion is the commitment to the God whom Christ reveals and the rejection of all idols of God, whether of our own or another's making.

Hallowed Be Thy Name (May Your Name Be Held Holy) In ancient cultures, name indicated inmost nature or essence; to know the name of something was to have control over it. It was daring of Moses to solicit God's name (Exodus 3:13–18); God answered Moses by giving the unpronounceable tetragrammaton, YHWH, a name regarded by Israel as so sacred that only once a year could it be uttered. A name, especially the name of a person, conveyed presence. Thus YHWH often is translated as "I Am Who Am" or "I will be with you."[9] The name of God is the covenant promise to be there (with Israel) always.

To hallow the name of God, to bless and sanctify God, means first of all to believe in the promise that God will be with us always. Second, faith is made concrete through praising, reverencing and glorifying the sacred name of God. The praise of God is the fulfillment of that for which we were made; according to Ephesians 1:12, "We who first hoped in Christ have been destined and appointed to live for the praise of God's glory" (cf. 2 Corinthians 3:18). God's holiness, God's name, is violated when those who claim to live in the name of God—for example, those baptized into the name of God—choose sin over praise. God's name is vindicated when we repent and are converted to the gospel. In addition to preset patterns of prayer, every aspect of our lives can become a doxology offered to the living God. By calling on the sacred name of God, we are, as Augustine suggests, praying for ourselves, "that what is always in itself holy (God) may be hallowed in [us]" (Sermon 6, 5).

Thy Kingdom Come   The reign of God (reign of heaven) was at the core of the preaching of Jesus. The reign has in some sense already arrived with Christ, but it is also a reality that is yet to be fully realized. According to the many parables in Matthew's gospel, the reign of heaven cannot be precisely located in any time or place; the reign is the establishment of God's love on earth, not the rule of a political monarch but the reign of grace and glory that triumphs over sin, death and Satan. By praying for the coming of the reign of heaven we affiliate ourselves with the action of God in history, which is a way of blessing the name of God.

Thy Will Be Done on Earth as It Is in Heaven   In the earliest church, this petition probably reminded Christians of the scene reported in Gethsemane when Jesus prayed, "Abba, Father, all things are possible to you; remove this cup from me; yet not what I will, but what you will" (Mark 14:36). What is God's will? How do we join our will with God's?

Cyprian of Carthage, a third-century African theologian, wrote in his commentary on the Lord's Prayer:

> Now, the will of God is precisely what Christ both did and taught. It entails being humble in our life-style, steadfast in our faith, modest in our words, just in our actions, merciful in our dealings, disciplined in our conduct, incapable of inflicting a wrong but able to bear one inflicted upon us; keeping peace with our brothers and sisters; loving God with all our heart, cherishing God as Father while fearing God as God.[10]

In other words, God's will is that we "be Christ" to one another. Joining our will to God's will does not mean slavish submission, not the expectation that we relinquish our own will by going against our humanity. Rather, our humanity is most perfectly realized when we do what Christ would have done, when we are persons in relationship to others just as Christ was in relationship (e.g., John 13:14; 15:12). Christ is called the image or icon of the invisible God (Colossians 1:15); we are enjoined to be icons of Christ.

To summarize the Lord's Prayer so far, the first three petitions are different forms of the same theme. That the name of God be glorified, that the reign of God be established and that the will of God be done — these three are one and the same divine action. Thus when we pray as Jesus taught the disciples, we give ourselves over to the power of the God whose history has been joined with our own. By praying the Lord's Prayer, we ask to be shaped and reshaped by the holy name of God who is the fountain of all holiness.

Give Us This Day Our Daily Bread   At this point, the prayer shifts away from the "heavenly" realm to the daily need for bread. This petition probably is related to the instruction that Jesus gives to go forth without provisions (Matthew 6:8) and without worry for tomorrow (Matthew 6:34).

"Bread" is that which is minimally necessary for life. Placing ourselves in the situation of hunger and need reminds us of our absolute dependence on God for every hair on our head, every breath we take. Praying for bread on a daily basis is an opportunity to scale down what we think we need to survive (Matthew 6:25–33). In the fourth century, Gregory of Nyssa wrote, apparently with a bit of exasperation:

> We were charged to say to God, "Give us our bread," and in this manner to pray simply for what is sufficient to sustain bodily life, not for opulence and wealth, not for rich robes of purple, not for golden jewelry and glistening gems, not for silver, not for an overabundance of property or anything of that sort, whereby the soul may be distracted from the incomparably more important endeavor to come to God but only for our daily bread.
>
> Can you perceive the depth of wisdom and the fund of instruction that this short word contains? Quite openly the Lord is calling to almost all who care to understand it: Stop making difficulties! It is little that you really need, as far as your human nature is concerned.[11]

Asking God for daily bread is a way of praying for all that we truly need in every realm: spiritual, material, intellectual, emotional. God already knows what we need because God is concerned with the smallest details of our lives, and God gives graciously and generously what we actually need.

> Therefore do not be anxious saying, "What shall we eat?" or "What shall we drink?" or "What shall we wear?" For the gentiles seek all these things; and your heavenly Father knows that you need them all. But seek first God's reign and God's righteousness, and all these things shall be yours as well. (Matthew 6:31–33)

Forgive Us Our Debts as We Also Have Forgiven Our Debtors This petition highlights the communitarian and social dimension of sin. Sin against one another is sin against God (see Matthew 5:23–24). The petition is not a *quid pro quo,* a request that God forgive us only in the measure that we forgive others. Rather, God's forgiveness of our own sin is the basis for our forgiveness of another. We can truly forgive each other only if we regard everyone as a brother or sister, not as an outsider or a threat to our person. Readiness to forgive entails letting go of the desire to judge the other.

God's judgment is based on love and mercy (cf. Luke 6:36–38); ours is to be the same (Matthew 5:48). When we forgive, we "in a certain sense become God" (Gregory of Nyssa) by showing the gradual conformity of our nature to God's. Still, there is an asymmetry between ours and God's forgiveness. In God, love and judgment are identical. Our identification with God, however, is located not in our capacity to judge others but in our capacity to love. Because we are loved, we are in a position to love but never to judge. The work of conversion is therefore the transformation of our judgment into love. When we forgive another, we become free to embrace the now–former enemy, to work actively to achieve her or his good, to respond no longer out of hurt or fear but from love (see Matthew 5:38–48).

Lead Us Not into Temptation (Do Not Put Us to the Test), But Deliver Us from Evil This final petition does not mean that the loving God whom we confidently address in the opening words of the Lord's Prayer intentionally leads us into temptation, sin and guilt. The early church expected some type of final eschatological trial (see Revelation 3:10) in which all the forces of evil would be marshaled against God but from which God would emerge triumphant. Matthew's text likely refers to this final tribulation.

At the same time, God created us for blessedness, holiness, life eternal. According to James 1:13–14, "Let no one say when he or she is tempted, 'I am tempted by God,' for God cannot be tempted with evil, and God tempts no one. But each person is tempted when he or she is lured and enticed by her or his own desire." Strictly speaking, it is not God who tempts, but other forces, hostile to love, that "put us to the test." Consequently, this part of the prayer ordinarily is interpreted to mean, "let us not succumb to," "do not abandon us to" or "let us not be led into evil." The prayer begs God to rescue us.

Praying this petition can be an occasion to acknowledge that often we are not in a position to know exactly what in our circumstances is a temptation to evil. Every aspect of our lives—poverty as well as wealth, ignorance as well as knowledge, sickness as well as health—*can be* a temptation away from hallowing God's name, praying for the reign of God and doing God's will. Evil is by its nature subtle. At times, we simply "fall into" sin. We are passively swept into it; for example, we remain silent rather than gently protest against an unkind remark. By the same token, grace is equally subtle and sublime; often we fail to recognize the presence of God in broken situations and imperfect decisions.

Only through constant prayer are we able to discern what is evil and be converted away from its hold on us. The holy man or woman has a discriminating eye for God's presence as well as for God's absence. The holy person is able to glimpse the extraordinary in the ordinary, to see the banality and emptiness of the glamorous. Praying that we not be abandoned to evil is therefore not a prayer for escape from the world but a prayer that we develop acute sensitivities to the many sin-filled and grace-filled dimensions of our existence.

Notes

[1] Tertullian, *De Oratione* 1:36.

[2] Thomas Aquinas, *Summa Theologiae* II-II, q. 83, a. 9.

[3] Cf. Raymond E. Brown, "The *Pater Noster* as an Eschatological Prayer," *Theological Studies* 22 (1961): 175–208, especially 178.

[4] Karl Rahner, *On Prayer* (New York: Paulist Press, 1958), 19. I have separated the lines to show the commentary more clearly, but the original reads in a continuous paragraph.

[5] Cf. Brown, "The *Pater Noster*," 202.

[6] Not until the fourth century, in the context of the trinitarian controversy, did theologians specify several other meanings of the word *Father:* the Unoriginated Origin, the Unbegotten, Father of the Son, Creator of the universe.

[7] Augustine, Sermon 8, 2

[8] If we address God as *Abba*/Father, we are using a term of intimacy that was a characteristic of Jesus' own prayer. "Father" expresses the personal and relational character of God. However, we must be careful not to let dogmatic positions outrun biblical evidence (cf. J. Barr, "Abba Isn't 'Daddy,'" *Journal of Theological Studies* 39 [1988]: 28–47), nor to confuse God's fatherhood with human fatherhood. In the fourth century, Gregory of Nazianzus ridiculed his opponents who thought that God was male because God is called Father, that the deity is feminine because of the gender of the word or that the Spirit is neuter because it does not beget. Gregory ruled out both philological and biological connotations; in one homily, he preached that God's fatherhood has nothing to do with marriage, pregnancy, midwifery or the danger of miscarriage (*De Oratione* 31, 7). Cf. also Catherine Mowry Lacugna, "The Baptismal Formula, Feminist Objections and Trinitarian Theology," *Journal of Ecumenical Studies* 26:2 (1989).

[9] J. C. Murray, *The Problem of God* (New Haven: Yale University Press, 1964), 8–10.

[10] Cyprian of Carthage, *Commentary on the Lord's Prayer,* 15, trans. by E. Bonin (Westminster MD: Christian Classics, 1983).

[11] Gregory of Nyssa, *Commentary on the Lord's Prayer;* see Karl Becker and Marie Peter, eds., *Our Father: A Handbook for Meditation,* trans. by Ruth Mary Bethell (Chicago: Henry Regnery Co., 1956), 240.

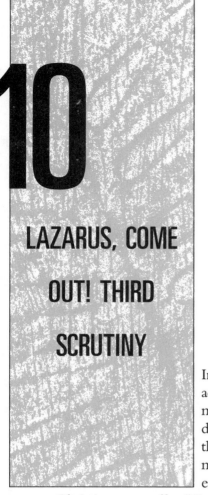

10

LAZARUS, COME OUT! THIRD SCRUTINY

In the gospel assigned to the rite of acceptance into the order of catechumens, John's disciples ask Jesus, "Where do you stay?" Jesus' answer is a phrase that, however often quoted, always remains fresh and new, a favorite among enthusiasts for the catechumenate[1] and among Christians generally: "Come and see."

The more this little phrase is polished, the more it shines. "Come and see" because it is useless to explain these things before you have undertaken to change the position from which you view them. "Come and you will see" because an adventure is about to begin and you can be a part of it if you choose to be. "Come and see" because no one else can see for you, and no one as wise as Jesus would presume to deprive you of the chance to see for yourself. The promise, the offer, the invitation: Jesus' first encounter with his first disciples in John's gospel encompasses all these things. Like the first disciples, the new catechumens and candidates come, and they "see" a great deal.

At a later stage in the initiation process, we again hear the words "come and see" in the gospel assigned to the liturgy of the third scrutiny. This time they are not addressed to the disciples, but to Jesus. This time they draw attention not to the

RITA
FERRONE

promise of life, but to the reality of death. The phrase appears in drab and somber clothing. It has taken on the aspect of a throwaway line— "come and see and have done with it"—a phrase perhaps not even intended by the evangelist to evoke that other, more portentous occasion on the banks of the Jordan River.[2] Yet for those who have lived with the invitation of Jesus in John 1:39, and who, thus invited, have at last come to the third and final scrutiny, the contrast between this and that other "come and see" is a poignant one. Jesus asks where his dead friend Lazarus is laid, and Martha and Mary and the Jews say to him: "Come and see."

Come and see the tomb. Come and see the place of death. Come and see the source of our grief, the irreversible human lot, the triumph of Satan, the negation of God's gift. In a certain sense, they are saying to Jesus, come and see where *we* live, where our destiny takes us all in the end. Come and meet the opponent whom we spend our lives denying and fighting, inevitably to lose. Come and see what we mourn over now for Lazarus, yet what also is always near at hand for us all.

The third scrutiny invites us into the mystery of ultimate defeats and ultimate victories. It seeks to reveal the presence of death-dealing forces, terminal illnesses and fatal attractions in ourselves, our church and our world,[3] and to reaffirm the hope of abundant and eternal life offered by Jesus. The drama of the raising of Lazarus is found in the confrontation and defeat of the kingdom of death by God through the word and deed of Jesus.

The Ritual

The Name of the Rite   In implementing the catechumenate, a certain amount of attention must be given to explaining unfamiliar language. In the case of the scrutinies, the very name occasions the question "Who is scrutinizing whom?" Some may wonder: Is this some form of public confession in which the church examines the sins of the elect? To allay the understandable anxiety of all involved—lest it appear that the church is scrutinizing the elect—a sincere effort often is made to emphasize that the elect scrutinize themselves.

If the misconception is a wild distortion, the explanation is, unfortunately, something of a reduction. A scrutiny is more than an exercise in self-awareness and is very different from submitting one's conduct to the judgment of the church. Better to say that Jesus is the one who scrutinizes the elect, whom he loves and has called to himself. Because he loves them he would have them "search their own consciences" (RCIA, 139) and he would have them be "instructed gradually about the mystery of sin, from which the whole world and every person longs to be delivered" (RCIA, 143). The church has a role, and the participation of the elect themselves is essential, but the center of the event is the action of God in Christ Jesus, which, however much it discloses to us about ourselves, never is only about us. The scrutiny in a fundamental sense is about God and God's self-revelation in Jesus Christ.

The Shape of the Rite   The rite of the third scrutiny is straightforward, simple and exactly the same in structure as the previous two scrutinies. As in the first two, the rite requires the Year A readings. The litany of intercession should be adapted to reflect the actual concerns of the elect. Later in the liturgy, the elect and their godparents are remembered in the eucharistic prayer. The texts of the exorcism prayers are sound as they stand. The structure of the ritual is solid: litany, prayer to God the Father, imposition of hands in silence, prayer to Christ with hands outstretched over the elect. Done with appropriate solemnity, it bears the weight of the occasion quite well just as it is.

A Passive Role?   A criticism sometimes leveled against the scrutinies is that they, more than any of the other initiation rites, render the elect passive.[4] This observation is to some extent true. The elect do not speak in the rite. Neither do their godparents speak for them or about them to the assembly. The concerns of the elect may find their way into the litany, but anonymity is preserved for obvious reasons. We pray for them and lay hands on them. That is all.

The one thing asked of the elect (besides the minor requirement that they assume some humble posture, such as kneeling) is that they surrender to the grace of God. Provided we allow that interior actions—thoughts, feelings, emotions—may be considered "doing something," we may ask: Is this surrender passive? And if so, isn't this kind of passivity tremendously worthwhile and important? It may not look like much on the dance floor, but it is undoubtedly the longest mile in the spiritual life.

The scrutinies are unlike the other major rituals of Christian initiation for good reason. The range and repertoire of our initiation rituals is wide and varied in order to serve a full expression of Christian conversion. The rites ritualize a wide variety of things: welcome, commitment, decision—also surrender, purgation, illumination and healing. The third scrutiny is the high-water mark of the latter kind of action. It would be foolish indeed to enter into a liturgy in which the main idea is to identify with a corpse and then to fret because it makes us out to be too passive.

Progressions in the Rite   The scrutinies are meant to have a progressive character, and even a cursory glance at the narrative material of the gospel texts shows a clear progression. It is bad to be thirsty, worse to be blind and worst of all to die. It is good to have one's thirst quenched, a greater gift to be blessed with sight, most blessed of all to have life.

One also might look at this as a progression in the way the elect invite Jesus in: to "come and see" my thirst, my blindness and, last of all, my dying. There is a progression also in seeing that God already has made springs flow in the deserts of human hearts, lifted the impenetrable darkness of sin and called forth life from the decay of death. We pray for a quickening of that saving grace that all believers have known and that already has begun to work within the elect.

The progressive nature of the three scrutinies[5] lends a weightiness to the last of these three public exorcisms. But even this scrutiny is incomplete, as the others are, because it looks forward to the Easter Vigil. The third scrutiny, in reading and prayer, proclaims that Jesus is the resurrection and the life. But the full impact of that message will not be felt until Easter. Just as the raising of Lazarus is a preparation for the resurrection of Jesus, so the third scrutiny is a preparation for the Easter Vigil when the elect will die and rise with Christ.

The Readings

All three readings of this liturgy are rich in material for preaching and catechesis: the vision of Ezekiel that culminates in God's promise to breathe life into God's people, who, in their exile, are as good as dead; the passage from Romans in which Paul relates sin to death and voices the promise of life that belongs to Christians because of what God has done in Christ; and the rich and complex story of the raising of Lazarus from the Gospel of John.

It would be too much to comment on all of these texts in the space of one chapter. The Lazarus story alone offers more material than can be explored thoroughly in these pages. The catechist and preacher who continue to search for new insights in these texts as they are used year by year deserve their reward and will not be lightly relieved of their burden by the following paragraphs. There are, nevertheless, two aspects of the story of the raising of Lazarus that I would like to point out and comment on here because I think that they may be fruitful starting points for reflection: Jesus' state of mind as he confronts the situation and the consequences of the miracle for Jesus himself.

Anger at Death In verse 33 (echoed in verse 38), the evangelist describes Jesus as he confronts the situation: "He was troubled in spirit, moved with the deepest emotions" *(New American Bible)*. "He was deeply moved in spirit and troubled" *(Revised Standard Version)*. ". . . in great distress, with a sigh that came straight from the heart . . ." *(Jerusalem Bible)*. ". . . he shuddered, moved with the deepest emotions" *(American Bible)*. I am persuaded by Raymond Brown's discussion of these verses[6] that the language used here very possibly expresses not sorrow or a more tender emotion, but anger at "manifestations of Satan's kingdom of evil."[7]

Far from being an aloof conjurer preparing to do his trick, or a warmhearted humanitarian motivated by sympathy for his neighbors over an unfortunate event, Jesus is a combatant engaged in a conflict that shakes him deeply. He is in a rage (albeit an articulate rage) over what he sees: death, Satan's last laugh, the negation of the gift of life.

Jesus' shudder and the deep emotion that stirs him are not explored in the story. We are not told their meaning, perhaps because we do not need to be told. I believe that all of suffering humanity knows that shudder. It is a common experience. Everyone who has ever been under the heel of oppression knows the deep emotion that interferes with our breathing. It requires no explanation. Yet it speaks to us powerfully of who Jesus is for us. He is God-with-us. He also is always *for* us.

I propose this as a starting point for reflection not so much because we should marvel at Jesus' capacity to feel the emotion of anger, but so that we should see his anger directed at death. This is an enormous consolation and a teaching. One is reminded, perversely, of all the platitudes that one hears on occasions of tragic or sudden death. How misguided, how utterly false to imagine that God willed this plane to crash, this boy to die because of a physician's mistake, this child to perish of AIDS. Even of the most peaceful and "natural" of deaths it seems unnatural to say "it was God's will," because the God we know in scripture is so much a God of the living.

Among the elect there may be some who have tried to take their own lives or who are morally responsible for the death of another, whether by violence, by an act of recklessness, by abortion or by malicious neglect. On another plane, we all share a certain complicity in social sin that results in death—people starve as we enjoy this "land of plenty," gun-control bills are defeated and the number of homicides in our cities continues to climb, diplomatic missions fail and 50,000 or more Iraqis and others are killed in war. We deal in death in less dramatic ways, too. It is possible to kill someone's reputation with slander, to "cut someone dead" with rejection, to destroy self-esteem with nagging criticism. In the scrutiny we pray not only to be delivered from death, as if human creatures are ever only its victims, but also to be delivered from the awful guilt of being the agent of death to one's neighbor, and even perhaps to one's self. If true repentance, sorrow for sins and amendment of life are all part of the catechumenate, they again will be stirred up and given deeper meaning by this story of Jesus, who is deeply moved in the face of death.

How have we experienced our God to be a God of life and of the living? What sign of this do we need most at this time in our lives? What are our reactions as we confront death and signs of death in our experience? Can we ask Jesus to confront death with us—in ourselves, in our all-too-human church and in our world?

Vital Consequences   The raising of Lazarus is described in the Gospel of John as the event that precipitates the plot to kill Jesus. As the story opens, we hear that Jesus is in danger of being stoned, but he decides to go to Bethany (about two miles from Jerusalem) despite this threat. In the story itself, Jesus' references to "glory" relate not only to the miracle that is about to be performed, but to the glory of his coming death and resurrection. Following this miracle is the scene in which Caiaphas delivers his memorable statement: "Do you not know that it is expedient that one man should die for the people?" (John 11:50), and the plan to put Jesus to death is formed. Inextricably bound up with the raising of Lazarus is Jesus' own journey to suffering and death.

Despite what seems to be Jesus' serene, superhuman knowledge of all this, again the image of conjurer could not be more wrong. Part of the essence of the magician's art is that his tricks cost him nothing. If they proved costly for him, the magic would be gone. Jesus' miracles, however, cost him his life. It is almost as if he agrees to trade places in the tomb with Lazarus, that symbol of all humanity, whom Jesus loves.[8]

Jesus raises the dead at other times, too (see Matthew 9:18 ff., Mark 5:35 ff., Luke 7:11 ff.), but this miracle, with its fatal consequences, is the one that is recalled as we near Holy Week. Our freedom is bought at a price (1 Corinthians 6:20). In the words of the Exsultet, "to ransom a slave, you gave away your Son." In a further twist of our natural expectations, this outcome is portrayed not as a horrible defeat but as a tremendous victory. What is going on here? Surely it would be blasphemous to suggest that God's only Son should be delivered up to death so that one person, or even so that all people, could get up out of their tombs and carry on as before. Something else must be intended. It must be that something new comes into the world because of this juggling of fates.

As the elect draw closer to Easter, they are being drawn into the very center of a new creation. The raising of Lazarus poses the question: How does a person live once it becomes clear that one's whole existence is a gift, a miracle? The elect are in the process of stepping into this existence, receiving this gift, becoming this miracle. Whatever it is, it is not the same as what came before. Sometimes it is called "life in Christ," sometimes "life in the Spirit." It has to do with being like Christ and bringing his kingdom into this world. It is something still being discovered, and its meaning will not be exhausted until Christ comes again in glory.

Conclusion

In Dostoyevski's novel *Crime and Punishment,* Raskolnikov's conversion turns on the story of the raising of Lazarus. The story is treasured up out of the heart of the young prostitute Sonia, whose existence is so wretched, it seems that only faith in a miracle keeps her from suicide. In what is one of the most powerful scenes in all literature, Raskolnikov roughly demands that Sonia read him the story.

She does read it to him, haltingly at first, her voice breaking, then becoming steady and gaining momentum. As she reads she becomes increasingly vibrant, powerful and expressive. The story reaches a crescendo, like a great wave breaking on the shore, and is over, but it is the beginning of Raskolnikov's long climb out of the pit of despair. It is after this scene that the decision to confess to the murder of the pawnbroker woman and her sister Lizaveta—the decision that saves him as a moral human being—begins to take shape.

How clear it is in the novel both that Raskolnikov needed to have Sonia read him that story and that she needed to read it to him. It is just as true—if not always so clear—that every human being who embarks on a way of conversion needs the testimony of witnesses who bear the gospel as their treasure. The story of the raising of Lazarus lives when it is passed on by someone who has found life in it.

The rite of the third scrutiny asks the church to read to the elect the story of the raising of Lazarus with conviction and with passion, as a living word from "the eternal book."[9] If we do this, it cannot but happen that when we pray over the elect, Jesus will say to them, in our own voices and with power, "Lazarus, come out!"

Notes

[1] Karen Albertus' catechetical program for adult initiation, *Come and See* (Cincinnati OH: St. Anthony Messenger Press, 1990), is one example; numerous "homegrown" resources echo this theme.

[2] In Greek, the phrases are not identical, as they are in English, but vary slightly in number and tense. Their practical meaning, however, is the same.

[3] Conversion is never a purely personal or private phenomenon. Jim Dunning treats the topic of social sin extensively and persuasively in his article, "Confronting the Demons: the Social Dimensions of Conversion," in *Conversion and the Catechumenate* (Mahwah NJ: Paulist Press, 1984).

[4] See, for instance, Kevin Hart's "The Rites of the Scrutinies and the Presentations" in *Christian Initiation Resources Reader,* vol. III (New York: Sadlier, 1984) 109, or Michel Dujarier, *The Rites of Christian Initiation,* (New York: Sadlier, 1979) 129.

[5] "From the first to the final scrutiny the elect should progress in their perception of sin and their desire for salvation." (RCIA, 143)

[6] Raymond E. Brown, "The Gospel According to John" (I -XII), in the *Anchor Bible,* vol. 29 (Garden City NY: Doubleday, 1966) 425, 426, 436.

[7] *Ibid.,* 426.

[8] The feeling of the remarkable reversal involved in Jesus' suffering and death is captured well in the words of Alexander Means's hymn: "What wondrous love is this, O my soul . . . What wondrous love is this that caused the Lord of bliss to bear the dreadful curse for my soul . . . ?"

[9] "The candle end was flickering out in the battered candlestick, dimly lighting up in the poverty-stricken room the murderer and the harlot who had so strangely been reading together the eternal book. Five minutes or more passed." Fyodor Dostoyevski, *Crime and Punishment,* trans. by Constance Garnett (New York: Bantam Books, 1958) 285.

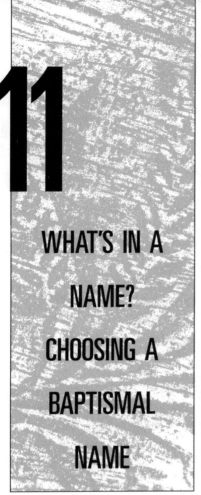

11

WHAT'S IN A NAME? CHOOSING A BAPTISMAL NAME

Shortly after my brother Michael—then in kindergarten—learned the intricacies of the sacrament of baptism, he started to baptize! His "catechumens" included a goodly number of our Jewish playmates in the neighborhood. Michael's ritual involved water and word, signing and the giving of a new name. It was this latter rite that had us nearly run out of the neighborhood: Rebecca became "Mary," Aaron would answer only to "James" and that evening at his dinner table, Phil announced, "Call me John." Interfaith dialogue suffered a catastrophic breakdown in the aftermath of Michael's zeal for souls.

Years later, this memory has surfaced as I begin a reflection on baptismal naming. Recollections at this distance are hazy, of course, but I remember puzzling over one curiosity: Folks seemed to be bothered more by the new name given to their offspring than by the fact that their children had been inducted, albeit quite innocently, into the Roman Catholic Church.

Our neighbors knew that the right to select a name belongs, in the first instance, to parents or guardians, and that others—particularly five-year-olds—have no right to usurp

KATHLEEN HUGHES

such authority. My brother's ritual naming of his friends had been a powerful symbol: a repudiation of one identity for another, a statement of new status, a source of alienation. A lot is in a name!

In some measure, the focus of this chapter is quite narrow. I have been asked to comment on the choice of a baptismal name and, in the process, to examine and interpret the following rubric:

> The rite of choosing a baptismal name may be celebrated on Holy Saturday, unless it was included in the rite of acceptance into the order of catechumens. The elect may choose a new name, which is either a traditional Christian name or a name of regional usage that is not incompatible with Christian beliefs. Where it seems better suited to the circumstances and the elect are not too numerous, the naming may consist simply in an explanation of the given name of each of the elect. (RCIA, 200)

My recollections from childhood, however, warn me that we should neither underestimate the power of naming nor decide too quickly to drop the preparation rites on Holy Saturday, or at least the naming opportunity of that day.

Accordingly, I will begin by exploring the giving or taking of a new name as that impulse has been interpreted in scripture and tradition. Second, I will review the change in canon law that has made the selection of a Christian name an option rather than a necessity. Third, I will develop the contemporary hesitations about the selection of a new name and propose what may underlie these cautions. And finally, I will attempt to situate the question of naming in its Holy Saturday context and suggest how "naming" might become an important ritual moment on the threshold of initiation.

A Historical Perspective

Names, in the scriptures, are not simply ways of distinguishing one person from another; they capture something of the mysterious and unique identities of the ones who are designated. To confer a name is to exercise authority; to know a name is a source of power; to utter a name is to make a disclosure about the character and the uniqueness of the one so titled.

Scriptural naming often acts as a controlling metaphor for the intimacy of divine-human interaction: "I have called you by your name; you are mine" (Isaiah 43:1); "See, upon the palms of my hands I have written your name" (Isaiah 49:16); "You shall be called by a new name pronounced by the mouth of the Lord" (Isaiah 62:2); "My servants shall be called by another name by which they will be blessed" (Isaiah 65:15). Such passages indicate Israel's belief in God's knowledge, authority, possession and election of the one whose name God knows, and that very knowledge implies a personal relationship with God.

Similarly, the giving of a *new* name in the scriptures generally is linked with a divine commission. Abram, Sarai, Jacob, Simon and numerous others receive a new name at a crossroads moment in their lives, and the name carries with it a deputation: father of a multitude of nations (Abraham), mother of nations (Sarah), the one who contended with God (Israel), rock and foundation (Peter). In a sense, it is the naming itself that entrusts its bearer with a mission, and human acceptance of a divine commission involves acceptance of "the name" bestowed by God. One might even paraphrase the words of the prophet: "I bore your name, O Lord" (Jeremiah 15:16) with the words "I have finished the work that you have given me to do."

To discover God's name for us is the work of a lifetime. The Book of Revelation speaks of the white stone on which is written the name known only by the recipient (Revelation 2:17), an image that implies that as we grow in our relationship with God and deepen our knowledge of God, we come to a deeper knowledge of the person God calls us to be. The name is known only to ourselves; it expresses our personal identity—all we are, our dreams, our hopes, our joys and sorrows, our limitations and our giftedness. Our identity is forged and personally appropriated through intimacy with the Holy One.

There is no evidence that the early community chose baptismal names when they embraced Christianity. The name that they received at their initiation was the name "Christian," the community's acknowledgment that these candidates were in relationship with Christ and had embraced Christ's mission. Occasionally, converts to Christianity in the early church added a second name to their given name to honor someone instrumental in the process of conversion, to place their lives under the patronage of an ancestor in the faith or to suggest a quality of life that they hoped to live, but the selection of a second name was optional, not legislated.

By the middle of the fourth century, Christians appeared to be more discriminating about the naming of their children, for example, naming their offspring after early confessors and martyrs, or selecting appropriate virtues, ideas and attitudes such as faith, salvation, blessed, reborn or peace. The names of prominent missionary apostles also seem to have been favored names in areas where they exercised their ministry. But there is no uniform practice apparent in historical records, nor does it yet appear that adult converts exchanged "pagan" names for Christian names.

The medieval compilation of martyrologies was yet another impetus to the choice of Christian baptismal names. In addition, pilgrimages, saints' legends, romances and morality plays all served to popularize the names of scriptural figures, martyrs and saints of the Church. After the Council of Trent decreed the orthodoxy of veneration of the saints—and indeed, promoted their cult—priests were directed to persuade Christian parents to select patron saints for their children. If parents insisted on another name, the priest was to add the name of a saint as a second baptismal name. This legislation was incorporated into the Code of Canon Law of 1917.

Two other historical traditions have some bearing on the question of changing one's name. The first is the papal prerogative, exercised apparently only from the sixth century, of selecting a new name on election to the See of Peter. Until the turn of the millennium, the selection of a new papal name was sporadic; since that time, only two popes have kept their given names. Little is written of this custom. The choice of a new name conveys the desire of the incumbent to place his pontificate under the patronage of one or several forebearers of the faith.

Over the course of time, the developing custom of conferring new names on religious may have exercised some influence on the selection of a papal name. Giving new names to men and women religious either at entrance into a community or at profession of vows also began around the sixth century. As with the pope, the candidate for religious life selected—or was given—the name of a patron whose life might be emulated. Religious naming also symbolized a spirituality of religious life: To receive a new name was to leave an old name behind; to embrace a new name was to cut oneself off from one's former way of life; to choose a new name was to leave the past behind, to die to one's worldly ways, to live no longer for oneself but for Christ. The new religious name and new identity also were symbolized by a different garb, a different style of life and so on.

Baptismal Naming in Canonical Perspective

The 1917 *Code of Canon Law* is quite unbending about the need for receiving a Christian name at baptism: "Pastors should see to it that the person to be baptized is given a Christian name; but if they are unable to fulfill this, they should add to the name given by the parents the name of some saint, and they should inscribe each name in the baptismal register" (761). In contrast, the 1983 code states: "Parents, sponsors and the pastor are to see that a name foreign to a Christian mentality is not given" (855).

There are some interesting contrasts between these two formulations. The earlier code gave both responsibility and authority in naming to the pastor. He either accepted parental choice or augmented their selection with the name of a saint or a Christian virtue if parents objected to his substitution. Not infrequently under the old code, parents were alienated from the church when pastors usurped parental authority in the bestowing of a name.

Current legislation suggests that the parents and sponsors share responsibility with the pastor for naming the candidate. The choice of a name is limited only by a negative norm: The name should not offend Christian sensibilities. Many neutral names, family names for example, now are acceptable, as are names appropriate to various regions and cultures. What formerly may have been regarded as a "pagan" or "non-Christian" name is now a moot point; only the obvious intention to offend Christian faith (an unimaginable condition in one approaching the Christian sacraments) or ignorance of anti-Christian values implied by a name would serve to eliminate the choice of a particular name in practice.

Both the directives in the *Rite of Christian Initiation of Adults* and the *Code of Canon Law* suggest that adult candidates may maintain the use of their given names and need not select a new baptismal name. In fact, according to the norms of the RCIA, only persons from cultures in which it is the practice of non-Christian religions to give a new name need consider receiving a new Christian name or a name familiar in the culture and compatible with Christian beliefs (RCIA, 73). In this way, the church recognizes indigenous cultural practices and values, and attempts to shape initiatory rites to local customs and expectations.

Taking a New Name — A Reassessment

The weight of scripture and tradition suggests that people at crossroads moments in their lives were given a new name or selected a name that would express the reality of their new being. While for centuries there was no legislation to mandate the choice of a Christian name, Christians seemed to gravitate in that direction. They selected, for themselves or for their children, patron saints whose lives were worthy of imitation. They named their children with words of hope and promise, with ways of being in the world. They gave their children the name of a confessor or a martyr as a way of keeping the memory of that person alive and as a way of honoring God's faithfulness in human history.

The choice of new names by popes and by women and men religious also reflected the desire to honor the memory of saints and to emulate the holiness of their lives. But, particularly for religious, a new name was also the symbol of flight from the world, from one's former way of life, from one's history, sometimes even from oneself. While there is ample scriptural precedent for the emptying of self and the declaration of death to the old person, and while religious profession ceremonies of the past could express this quite starkly through prostrations and palls, there is a new emphasis today in contemporary spirituality. Conversion does not imply denying one's past but bringing one's whole self before God: It is loved sinners who become loving servants. Conversion includes the discovery of the name God has called us to become. Conversion demands that we choose to be who we are at this moment and, day by day, to deepen our identity in communion with God. It is a person's name that expresses this being-in-process.

It is one's name that gathers up all one's identity, history and hopes. Perhaps one way to think anew about the process of Christian initiation is this: Initiation is the gradual process of discovery of the name God has called the candidate to be, and the candidate's acceptance of the relationship and the deputation that God's naming implies. This way of understanding the initiation process suggests a deeper appreciation of the way naming could function throughout the journey toward the Easter sacraments.

Naming in the Rites

Each of the threshold rites of the initiation process (i.e., the rite of acceptance into the order of catechumens and the rite of election) incorporates the naming of candidates. The gradual appropriation of one's name before God could function as a metaphor for the various stages of the conversion process. Clarity about the way this metaphor functions would lead to a certain care in the structuring of each of the threshold rites — not to give disproportionate emphasis to a secondary rite, but simply to allow one element in each of these rites to build over time from *giving one's name* to being *called by name* to *signing one's name* and then, in the preparatory rites of Holy Saturday, *explaining one's given name* on the eve of initiation. Let us look at these in turn.

The rite of acceptance into the order of catechumens begins with an invitation by the presider to each of the catechumens to tell the community her or his name (RCIA, 50). Sufficient time has preceded this threshold rite to evaluate a candidate's motives and dispositions; sufficient time also has preceded this moment so that the candidate approaches the threshold in self-possession, having recognized and responded to the stirrings of God who is calling her or him "by name." Making known their names is a first public disclosure of the catechumens' desire to know their own names—their identities before God—more deeply through prayer and the company and spirit of Christians. As candidates give their names to the community, they entrust themselves to these people gathered in welcome and allow the community a certain authority over their journeys from that point forward.

The second threshold, the election or enrollment of names, follows a "lengthy formation of the catechumens' minds and hearts" (118). Called an election because we celebrate God's choice of these men and women, this rite also incorporates an enrollment of names as the candidates' pledge of fidelity (119). While it is not specified in the rites or commentary, it might be presumed that it is fidelity to the Christian community's way of life—fidelity to the kerygma, to solitary prayer and worship in common, to the community's way of being in the world in mission—to which the candidates are pledging themselves. Fidelity also might be concretized as fidelity to relationships, to God above all and to the people God has elected and embraced as God's own.

Yet another way to understand fidelity might be intimately linked with the very act of enrolling one's name. The period of the catechumenate might be understood to be that time in which a candidate discovers the name written on the white stone. The significance of the white stone has been captured by George Macdonald, whose reflections are here paraphrased: A true name expresses character, nature, being and *meaning*. A name is a person's symbol—a soul picture—a sign that belongs to that one and no one else. Who but God can give such a name? No one but God sees who one is; no one but God, seeing, could express in a name-word that sum and harmony of all that God sees. Only when one has overcome, when one has become the name that God has given, does God give the stone, for only then would we understand what the name signifies (*Creation in Christ* [Wheaton, Illinois: H. Shaw Publishers, 1976], 237).

What a sublime way to think of the process of conversion throughout the catechumenate! What a wonderful context for understanding the pledge of fidelity that a catechumen makes in signing his or her name. What a fine way to conceive of the catechumenate, namely, as that period within which I discover my name—myself—most deeply as I am drawn into the heart of God and God's desire for me.

Once elected, candidates enter their long retreat to ponder the ways of God. And on the morning of their initiation, they gather for preparatory rites when *some explanation of their given names* might be appropriate. Here the potential richness of this directive is clear. The ritual invites the elect to ponder their deepest identities and, as appropriate, to engage in a period of faith-sharing with one another and with their sponsors. To *explain their names* at this stage is to attempt to disclose the wonders of God's love, for it is God alone who calls by name, who discloses one's name throughout a lifetime of fidelity, who invites the acceptance of the name as sacrament of this divine-human relationship.

Conclusion

The preparation rites on Holy Saturday often are regarded as secondary rites and quite impractical celebrations in a community gearing up for the mother of all vigils. When they are celebrated at all, the focus tends to converge on the return of the creed and on the ephphetha rite.

The purpose of these reflections has been to suggest a reconsideration of the preparatory rites in the larger context of the meaning of naming throughout the rites of Christian initiation. In the last analysis, "choosing a baptismal name" is God's prerogative for each of those whom God elects. On the morning of Holy Saturday, candidates for baptism might well spend some time with one another rejoicing that their names already are written in heaven (Luke 10:20).

Authors

Rita Ferrone is the former director of the Office of the Catechumenate for the archdiocese of New York. She also serves as a team member for institutes of the North American Forum on the Catechumenate.

Kathleen Hughes, RSCJ, is professor of pastoral liturgy at Catholic Theological Union in Chicago.

Edward Foley, Capuchin, is associate professor of liturgy and music at Catholic Theological Union in Chicago.

Mark R. Francis, CSV, is assistant professor of liturgy at Catholic Theological Union in Chicago.

Michael Joncas is a priest of the archdiocese of St. Paul–Minneapolis. He is a member of the theology faculty at the University of St. Thomas in St. Paul, Minnesota.

Catherine Mowry Lacugna is associate professor of systematic theology at the University of Notre Dame in Notre Dame, Indiana.

Marguerite Main is a pastoral associate at St. Louise Parish in Bellevue, Washington. She is a former chairperson of the Steering Committee of the North American Forum on the Catechumenate.

James Moudry is a consultant in liturgy and sacramental practice. He is the executive director of the Institute for the Christian Initiation of Children.

Ronald A. Oakham, O. CARM., is director of institutes for the North American Forum on the Catechumenate in Arlington, Virginia.